MUSLIM ETHICS: EMERGING VISTAS

Muslim Ethics:
Emerging Vistas

Amyn B. Sajoo

I.B. Tauris *Publishers*
LONDON • NEW YORK
in association with
The Institute of Ismaili Studies
LONDON

Published in 2004 by I.B.Tauris & Co Ltd
6 Salem Rd, London w2 4bu
175 Fifth Avenue, New York ny 10010
www.ibtauris.com

in association with The Institute of Ismaili Studies
42–44 Grosvenor Gardens, London sw1w oeb
www.iis.ac.uk

In the United States of America and in Canada distributed by
St Martin's Press, 175 Fifth Avenue, New York ny 10010

isbn 1 85043 550 2
ean 978 1 85043 550 1

A full cip record for this book is available from the British Library
A full cip record for this book is available from the Library of Congress

Library of Congress catalog card: available

Typeset in Minion Tra by Philip Armstrong on behalf of The Institute of
Ismaili Studies

Printed and bound in Great Britain by mpg Books Ltd, Bodmin

The Institute of Ismaili Studies

The Institute of Ismaili Studies was established in 1977 with the object of promoting scholarship and learning on Islam, in the historical as well as contemporary contexts, and a better understanding of its relationship with other societies and faiths.

The Institute's programmes encourage a perspective which is not confined to the theological and religious heritage of Islam, but seeks to explore the relationship of religious ideas to broader dimensions of society and culture. The programmes thus encourage an interdisciplinary approach to the materials of Islamic history and thought. Particular attention is also given to issues of modernity that arise as Muslims seek to relate their heritage to the contemporary situation.

Within the Islamic tradition, the Institute's programmes seek to promote research on those areas which have, to date, received relatively little attention from scholars. These include the intellectual and literary expressions of Shi'ism in general, and Ismailism in particular.

In the context of Islamic societies, the Institute's programmes are informed by the full range and diversity of cultures in which Islam is practised today, from the Middle East, South and Central Asia, and Africa to the industrialized societies of the West, thus taking into consideration the variety of contexts which shape the ideals, beliefs and practices of the faith.

These objectives are realised through concrete programmes and activities organised and implemented by various departments of the Institute. The Institute also collaborates periodically, on a programme-specific basis, with other institutions of learning in the United Kingdom and abroad.

The Institute's academic publications fall into a number of inter-related categories:

1. Occasional papers or essays addressing broad themes of the relationship between religion and society in the historical as well as modern contexts, with special reference to Islam.
2. Monographs exploring specific aspects of Islamic faith and culture, or the contributions of individual Muslim thinkers or writers.
3. Editions or translations of significant primary or secondary texts.
4. Translations of poetic or literary texts which illustrate the rich heritage of spiritual, devotional and symbolic expressions in Muslim history.
5. Works on Ismaili history and thought, and the relationship of the Ismailis to other traditions, communities and schools of thought in Islam.
6. Proceedings of conferences and seminars sponsored by the Institute.
7. Bibliographical works and catalogues which document manuscripts, printed texts and other source materials.

This book falls into category two listed above.

In facilitating these and other publications, the Institute's sole aim is to encourage original research and analysis of relevant issues. While every effort is made to ensure that the publications are of a high academic standard, there is naturally bound to be a diversity of views, ideas and interpretations. As such, the opinions expressed in these publications must be understood as belonging to their authors alone.

Table of Contents

Preface   ix

1. Taking Ethics Seriously: *Adab* to Zygotes   1

2. Civility and its Discontents   25

3. A Humanist Ethos: The Dance of Secular and Religious   47

4. Pluralist Governance   72

Appendices
A. The Charter of Medina (622 CE)   94
B. *The Aga Khan Development Network:*
   An Ethical Framework   99
C. Excerpts from *The Islamic Code of Medical Ethics*   108

   Notes   118
   Select Bibliography   153
   Index   158

Preface

When I proposed as the cover image of this volume the 16th-century Mughal depiction of 'Noah's Ark', the sponsors of the project as well as the publishers were briskly unanimous in sharing my enthusiasm. No doubt the near-universality of the underlying epic, whether in the Islamic and Judaeo-Christian traditions or the more diffuse archetypes of global cultures, has intense resonance for its celebration of rescue and redemption in an encounter with catastrophe. What could be more appropriate in a contemporary discussion of ethics, especially in an Islamic context, than affirming the core values of preserving life and solidarity across boundaries of class, culture and species?

Yet, the depiction offers up some subtly compelling themes that only hint at their own import, beckoning the viewer to the lush image and – like the serene figures on the upper deck – to a reflective engagement in the unpacking of meanings. Consider the sheer diversity of life in the vessel where humans are far outnumbered by the birds and animals, and the humans themselves come from various walks of life. No overt religious symbols appear in their midst, even though the depiction stems from a scriptural narrative: God's message to the Prophet Nuh (Noah) to salvage life from the Flood (detailed in the Qur'an, 11:25–49). Rather, secular and sacred are in easy confluence. The dragon-motif of the vessel itself is a popular borrowing from

Chinese tradition, recalling a pluralist impulse that imbues 'Islamic' art.[1] That impulse is only buttressed by the shared scriptural roots of the narrative itself.

Then there is the dynamic of action and contemplation, of deck-hands, rescuers and serene conversationalists partaking in a collective venture that is located within the narrative. Hence, the divine command to Nuh does not transform itself into passive compliance. Rather, the interplay of human agency and reason give meaning here to the normative by turning it into a lived ethos of stewardship, and beyond. Indeed, it is this agency and reason in action that lends substance to a claim on behalf of the sacred in an otherwise worldly setting. The basis of that agency and reason may be traced to multiple sources: to texts, perhaps like the Qur'an, that affirm the idea of solidarity, but also to social practices and precepts of the *umma* or community, and its articulations thereof in a variety of media, from painting and poetry to architecture.

In other words, the Mughal image of the Ark does not merely ensue from the religious narrative, but is also a 'source' of the affirmation of Nuh and his ethos at a given moment in the lived historical experience of Muslims. This is only reinforced by the absence of symbols of stately power and of formal religion. If the painting makes any statement – and one is inclined to hold that it does – then it must surely relate to the *moral* universe of the artist or his patron. As such, it transcends the mundane without losing sight of it. Thus, it captures variations in dress and social status, but pointedly subordinates these to the contingency of the whole: the animals and birds enjoy no less succour than the elites.[2] Again, the balance of pragmatism (among the deck-hands and rescuers) and reflection (among the conversationalists) is as acute as the poise of the vessel itself on the turbulent waters. The salvage is portrayed not only as that of members of various species, but also of the natural order of life itself – its energy, repose and ethical teleology.

'Men do not fathom intellectual history,' observes Owen Chadwick, 'if they ask about nothing but the intellect.'[3] After all, social contexts have everything to do with the warp and woof of intellectual expressions, and there is no reward in ignoring those seed-beds. Much the same is true of Muslim ethics: their study cannot usefully be confined to scripture and its attendant normative regime, even as it extends to scholarly commentaries in disciplines ranging from law and philosophy to the natural sciences. The foundational importance of these elements is axiomatic, for they offer tenets, arguments and stories that can be timeless in their potency – like the epic of Nuh's Ark. Yet the central role for Muslim ethics at large of the Qur'an and the body of prophetic guidance and conduct, the *Sunna*, is accompanied by a key principle, one that underlies the oft-repeated assertion about Islam being 'a way of life'. It is the idea of the historical locus of the life of Muhammad, with its series of well-documented struggles to fulfil a prophetic mission in which the pursuit of ethical ideals is not an abstraction but a practical matter. This is reflected in the sensibility of the founding Shi'i and Sunni ethical discourses of Miskawayh (932–1030), al-Ghazali (1058–1111) and Nasir al-Din Tusi (1201–74), among others.

Yet there have always been among us Muslims and non-Muslims who prefer to treat religious texts as bearing singular and fixed meanings, the life of the Prophet Muhammad as closed to the creative interpretation that it so richly merits, and the diverse histories of Muslims as a unitary history of 'Islam'. This perspective yields, predictably enough, an ethos that is readily identified as a body of sacred rules, some finding their way into law or *fiqh*, and the rest into the wider Shari'a as a normative expression of what Islam is. Applying this ethos to the daily challenges that confront a Muslim is, then, an act of *will*, albeit with discernment as far as identifying the relevant principles are concerned.

It is not only those of a 'fundamentalist' persuasion – better referred to as political Islamists – who adopt that view, in which human agency and reason are subordinated to acts of compliance. Ironically, that ideological posture is shared by numerous commentators on 'Islam' who, like the Islamists that they tend to be obsessed with, would rather not grapple with the intricacies of pluralist Muslim worlds, historical and contemporary, textual and social, orthodox and heterodox, and all the shades in between such binaries. That reductive tendency has rarely been as conspicuous as it is today, in the aftermath of the events of September 11, 2001. Vexing issues of political violence, tolerance, the nexus of individual and community, even the fresh challenges of biotechnology, are too loudly treated as if the ethical problems at hand have ready-made solutions that only need uncovering in scripture. Alas, the decibel level at which ideological Islam is proclaimed by a militant minority is echoed by observers – scholarly and journalistic – eager to 'explain' the conduct of political Islamists at face value, which surely is how commentators with any degree of sophistication are *not* supposed to commentate.

Talal Asad's seminal work, *Formations of the Secular,* notes the contradictions inherent in this legacy of Orientalist understandings of Islam (whose attentive audience has included Muslims themselves, taken by the authoritative, 'modernist' aura of that genre), which not only misconstrues the complexity of 'Islam' but also of 'religion' and its ethical life in the public and private spheres.

> A magical quality is attributed to Islamic religious texts, for they are said to be both essentially univocal (their meaning *cannot* be subject to dispute, just as 'fundamentalists' insist) and infectious (except in relation to the orientalist, who is, fortunately for him, immune to the their dangerous power). In fact in Islam as in Christianity there is a complicated history of shifting interpretations, and the distinction is recognized between the divine text and human approaches to it. Those who think that the motive for violent action lies in 'religious ideology' claim that any concern for the consequent suffering requires that we support the censorship of religious discourse... But it is not always clear whether it is pain and suffering as such that the secularist cares about or the pain and suffering that can be attributed to religious violence, because that is pain the modern imaginary conceives of as gratuitous.[4]

Among the principal burdens of this study is the claim that it is motivation that makes religious ethics in general, and Muslim ethics in particular, an exciting field of study amidst the advent of secular modernity. This is not about an exploration of how one attributes motive and responsibility to an actor in ethics (as compared with law, for example), and least of all about the psychology of motive-formation in its interface with social and private ethical action. Those are vast and indubitably relevant fields that merit attention in their own right. What I have chosen to address is a fundamental problem in approaches to modern ethical conduct that straddles easy divides between 'secular' and 'religious' motivation, and not only among

Muslims: it has to do with the question, 'Why act ethically?' Bernard Williams has shown how modern ethical theories are blinkered by failing to ask this question, and focusing instead on the what and how of ethics alone.[5]

Responding coherently to that query requires one to consider various conceptions of the 'good' in settings that are private and public, socio-political and scientific, past and present. It seems to me that asking whether an act is 'inherently' right or wrong as the primary question, and building an approach thereon in terms of secular or religious perspectives,[6] is to keep on the blinkers that Williams has exposed. When wedded to an adamantly secular framework, this gives short shrift at the outset to the discourses and praxis that religious affinities bring to the ethical choices that individuals actually make.

That deficit is surely fatal when it comes to the Muslim world (or other non-occidental societies), where the Durkheimian prevalence of the secular has played itself out so differently than in Europe and North America. Equally, an adamantly absolutist frame of reference, secular or religious, to whether something is inherently wrong, gives short shrift to the complexities of human motivation that attend such judgments in the real world. It reduces the interplay of reason and faith or commitment to nothing more than passive compliance within an impoverished, deus ex machina view of the world. Both frameworks exist for some, of course, but they can hardly tell the whole story.

In seeking, then, to do justice to contending and plural realities, I have ventured in the opening section to consider an array of social settings in which Muslim conceptions of the good have developed and are today unfolding, including biomedicine and ecology. Asking how and why those conceptions are to be taken seriously is the underlying thread that connects the settings, yielding continuities and reinventions of tradition and reason. Next, I focus successively on three distinct yet overlapping domains – of 'civility', 'humanism' and 'governance' – that compel our attention in normative and empirical terms alike. For they engage such basic contemporary notions as human rights, the rule of law and civic culture in which conceptions of the good, whether as ethos or specific moral judgments, are vitally entwined. Engaging with those notions, as indeed with the history of ethics generally, also requires acknowledging the continual entwining of 'Islamic' perspectives with those of other traditions, confessional and secular, which is rendered all the more necessary today amid globalization and the enormous diasporic presence of Muslims across civilizations. In turn, this reinforces the imperative of intercultural dialogue to mediate the collision of traditional identities with what Akbar Ahmed calls the 'post-honour' codes of modernity.[7]

As alluded to earlier, I have sought to range beyond sources and contexts that usually receive attention in such studies; hence, the canvas includes references to cultural expressions like novels, the cinema and fine art in which conceptions of the ethical are embedded. Perhaps that will come as no surprise in light of the cover image, with its irrepressible reminder that there is more to scripture than scripture itself. Emerging vistas evoke the supple nature of ethical questing that is captured by a character in Naguib Mahfouz's *Arabian Nights and Days*: 'It is an indication of truth's jealousy that it has left people running in the deserts of perplexity and drowning in the seas of doubt; and he who thinks he has attained it, it dissociates itself from him, and he who thinks he has dissociated himself from it has lost his way.'[8] Hence, we are reminded of the manner in which artistic genres can contribute to bridging the complex truths of normative texts and empirical reality, in the construction of narratives and meanings where we must take ethics seriously.[9]

Most of the writing of this study was undertaken at McGill University, Montreal, where Dean Barry Levy of the Department of Religious Studies arranged for me to spend the spring and summer of 2003 as Visiting Scholar. Quite apart from the gracious physical spaces that facilitated the reflection, research and writing, I had the support of the academic and administrative staff of the faculty and the wider McGill community, including some memorably rewarding conversations with Professors Margaret Somerville, Gregory Baum, Üner Turguay and Barry Levy.

At The Institute of Ismaili Studies (IIS) in London, Dr Farhad Daftary and Kutub Kassam commissioned and stewarded robust editorial support for this study. Indeed, the inception of the project lay in the prompting of Kutub Kassam during my affiliation with the

IIS as a Visiting Research Fellow (2000–01). It was then as well that the precursor to the essay here on 'Civility and its Discontents' was developed, for which I record my further appreciation. Nadia Holmes at the IIS lent her usual professionalism to the editing process. Linda Adams, June Marvel and Liz Banuelos at the Middle East Center at the University of Utah, Salt Lake City, kindly facilitated early access to the cover image, while Patricia Salazar picked up that ball skilfully at the IIS.

I was encouraged along the path of this study by Dr Abdallah Daar, Professor of Public Health and Surgery, and a director at the Centre for Bioethics, University of Toronto. His sensitivity to emerging issues in Muslim biomedical ethics is nothing short of remarkable, as is his capacity to shepherd the work of numerous new as well as established scholars in this broad and recondite field, from Europe and North America to the Middle East and South Asia. For his generosity of intellect and spirit in commenting on a draft of the opening essay, I am suitably grateful.

Professor Donald Grayston, director of Simon Fraser University's Institute of the Humanities, Vancouver, invited me to deliver a talk in March 2003 that developed into the third essay here, 'A Humanist Ethos: The Dance of Secular and Sacred'. For the stimulus of an occasion that spawned deliberation on comparative civic ethics in Muslim and Christian historical experience in the wake of September 11, 2001, and its aftermath, I am indebted to this Institute.

The essay on 'Pluralist Governance' was the upshot of a lecture that I delivered at the University of Victoria, British Columbia, at a community event to cap the 2003 annual meeting of the American Council for the Study of Islamic Societies (ACSIS). I thank Dean Andrew Rippin, Professor Arif Babul and Professor Conrad Brunk, director of the Centre for the Study of Religion and Society, all of the University of Victoria, who jointly extended the invitation to what for me was a most fruitful encounter.

Finally, I acknowledge the permission extended by The Institute of Ismaili Studies, Oxford University Press (Pakistan) and the Islamic Organization for Medical Sciences to reproduce the contents of the three appendices to this study.

These are but some of the collaborators and interlocutors without whom this study would not have materialized. They bear no responsibility, of course, for its shortcomings.

ABS
Vancouver
April, 2004

Chapter 1

Taking Ethics Seriously:
Adab to Zygotes

'If there is to be an invitation to morality, it will have to be toward concrete and accessible rules, not toward some abstract ideas that bend to any conceivable form yet solve no specific moral dilemma.'

Abdolkarim Soroush, *Reason, Freedom, and Democracy in Islam*[1]

'[T]he ethical individual dares to employ the expression that he or she is his own editor, but he is also fully aware that he is responsible for himself personally ... responsible to the order of things in which he lives, responsible to God.'

Søren Kierkegaard, *Either/Or: A Fragment of Life*[2]

I

In asserting that an act is authentically moral only in terms of the intention that accompanies it – unsullied by self-interest or 'mock virtues' – the Muslim philosopher Nasir al-Din al-Tusi (1201–74) anticipated Kant by over five centuries.[3] The harmony of outward and inner disposition and character was of the essence, both for the quality of the act itself and, ultimately, for the health of the soul. The Prophet Muhammad had, after all, proclaimed the primacy of

1

moral intent over all else, including legal obligation.[4] It is true that this perspective is shared among the major traditions of faith-based ethics. Yet, in the merging of sacred and secular that became the leitmotif of Muslim civilizational experience, the congruence of external and internal universes of meaning also bridged the moral choices of the individual and the community (*umma*). As al-Tusi, al-Farabi (879–950) and other Muslim thinkers saw it, often in an Aristotelian vein, individual happiness and virtue were premised on a life of association.[5] A reasoned account of the good and why it should be pursued must, then, repose on the quality of interaction of the personal and societal. 'Let there be among you', proclaims the Qur'an, 'a community that calls to the good (*al-khayr*), bidding virtue (*ma'ruf*) and forbidding vice (*munkar*)' (3:104). Rooted in '*arafa*, that which is known, the term *ma'ruf* signifies the social transparency of the idea of virtue.[6]

The ethos that emerges from scripture, whether through narratives or injunctions, is of necessity about the practical unfolding of moral principles: ideals and their implications are set forth within the bounds of the relationship among the individual, society and the divine. Layers of meaning attach themselves through the course of history to those ideals, and to the nature of the threefold relationship within which they are to be realized. In Islam, the primary ethical corpus derived from Qur'anic and prophetic direction and, additionally for the Shi'a, the guidance of designated Imams, is interwoven with literary and social mores (*adab*), as well as a robust intellectual tradition of which al-Tusi, Miskawayh (932–1030), al-Ghazali (1058–1111), Ibn Rushd (1126–89) and Fakhr al-Din al-Razi (1149–1209) are exemplars. Even the Shari'a, often thought of as a body of law, is foremost an encompassing ethos derived over time from the primary sources – of which legal norms (*fiqh*) derived in pluralist fashion are only a part.[7] Thus, the ethical tradition of Islam finds rich expression in the plenitude of virtually a millennium-and-a-half of historical experience.

Yet the picture is incomplete, for it does not convey the sense of the quotidian, the ordinary encounter of community and individual with moral choices, large and small. This is not merely about the relationship between 'ideals' and 'realities', which after all is integral to human frailty and pervades all normative systems. Rather, it is about recognizing that the tenets or ideals themselves are framed in the crucible of human experience, amid the congruence and tension of the demands of intellect, faith and tradition. After all, that is why scriptures find compelling expression in narratives that echo across the boundaries of culture, time and space.[8] Creation, death, sacrifice and love are staples of narrative and norm in the Bhagavad Gita and the Upanishads, the Hebrew and Christian Testaments, the Qur'an – as well as of cultural epics such as those of Gilgamesh, Manas and Homer's Odyssey. Their parables generate and impart human context to the norms which they proclaim, weaving sacred and secular into lived experience. The same is true of the spaces – physical and psychological – in which that experience unfolds.

Less majestically, oral as well as written narratives of daily experience that are part of our shared heritages capture the *detail* of lifeworlds in which religio-ethical principles are mediated by the mundane exigencies of moral choice by individuals, families and communities. Thus, the Qur'an's normative universe is given specificity by Muhammad's pragmatic engagement with vexing moral problems as captured in the Hadith tradition.[9] *Adab* often captures this sense of the 'empirical', not only in popular tales like *Kalila wa Dimna*, the *Maqamat* of al-Hariri and *Hayy Ibn Yaqzan*,[10] but also in the behavioural codes of artisans, calligraphers, musicians and painters.[11] One is mindful too of the informal conventions that were a conspicuous part of early Islam, like the *shari'a ummiya*, the 'unlettered code' that was interwoven with its scripted counterpart. There are hymnal narratives of mystical or devotional bent, always bearing an ethos and sometimes affirming a specific set of ethical norms; examples in Arabic, Persian and a host of Indic languages include *ghazal*, *qasida*, *qawwali* and *ginan*.[12] Modern secular chronicles can convey and influence the ethical sensibilities of the Muslim public square, as in the novels of Naguib Mahfouz, Orhan Pamuk, Tayib Salih, Ahdaf Soueif and M.G. Vassanji.[13] Their characters are as familiar as the difficult choices that they encounter in settings or states of mind where Islam is at the epicentre – lending credence to the notion that the deepest truths are perhaps located in fiction. To which can be added the impact of contemporary cinematic culture, as purveyor of 'common' and 'elite' values alike as they reflect as well as mould social identities. Post-revolutionary Iranian cinema is a prime instance, with the forthright yet subtle handling of the most serious philosophical issues by *auteurs* who have endured first-hand the vicissitudes of radical social and political change.[14]

Taking ethics seriously implies coming to terms with the variegated social canvas on which reasoned accounts of right and wrong are played out; it cannot be about the abstractions of moral theory or divine commands alone. The latter approach would amount to a retreat into what Abdolkarim Soroush calls 'the ethics of the Gods', where the palpable sense of the mundane that humans must inhabit is altogether lacking.[15] This is not to gainsay the rewards of delving into the primary sources for renewed inspiration, in this as in earlier epochs. Soroush, Khaled Abou El Fadl, Mohammed Arkoun, Sohail Hashmi, Ebrahim Moosa and others have been at the forefront of such endeavour – to recall the late Fazlur Rahman – as an exercise in *rational* historical retrieval that aims to grasp an ethical unity beyond 'isolated commands and injunctions'.[16] This effort, in contrast to what is commonly referred to as 'fundamentalist' or 'Islamist' revivalism, is firmly anchored in historicity and context: the past is not for imitation (*taqlid*) but part of a continuum in which texts, narratives and experience are shared by a diverse *umma*. Moreover, it is worth recalling that the *umma* was conceived not as an abstract ideal but a real entity with all 'the complexity and ambiguity of actual communities, religious or otherwise'.[17] As such, it was enjoined by the Qur'an to be more than a nominal *umma muslima* and to merit the status of the 'best community' by affirming right conduct (3:110).

This intertwining of the individual and communal selves is firmly grounded in the way that ethical life is actually constructed. For the narrative of an individual's life is tied invariably to an interlocking set of narratives that involve others, notes the moral philosopher Alasdair MacIntyre.[18] 'I can only answer the question "What am I to do?" if I can answer the prior question "Of what story or stories do I find myself a part?"'[19] The atomized, much less the disembodied, self is hardly a meaningful subject on which to build an edifice of right and wrong that has enduring practical relevance. This is implicitly recognized by religious traditions, where the individual is embedded in a larger whole: *re-ligare*, 'to bind together', is the font for 'religion'. Islam has made it pivotal to its scriptural as well as civilizational thrust. In the merging of secular and sacred, as well as the interlocking lives of the individual and the *umma*, Muslims recognize intuitively that faith traditions are the 'primary models for lived ethics':

> Religious ethics are distinguished by their grounding in the histories, texts, rituals, practices, and institutions of particular communities. Religion confronts philosophy with real life. Religion also confronts real life with philosophy. In and through religious narratives and rituals, people set everyday duties, concerns, conflicts, and hopes in a larger context, giving them meaning and significance beyond their own times and places.[20]

What this points to is a key divergence in the approach to the subject between most modern philosophy and religion. The former offers elaborate theories – stressing consequences, a social contract, social justice, human nature, and the like – that purport to be grounded in ideas either of what we ought to do as a moral duty (deontology) or what we should do to maximize social happiness (teleology). These theories purport to give us coherent responses to Socrates' observation that the unexamined life is not worth living. Aristotle, like an array of Eastern sages before him, sought to give both deontological and teleological answers to Socrates' question,[21] for in their cultural universes the unity of the individual and the community was not yet sundered. Their rationalist humanism was to profoundly shape early Muslim thought, which in the hands of Ibn Rushd (1126–98) attained fresh heights in the nexus of faith and reason – that in turn influenced the rebirth of European philosophy.[22] Yet if this rationalist thrust came to be muted in Muslim religious discourse amid the rise of conservative theology (*kalam*), the opposite was to occur in Occidental thought. 'What am I to do?' was less about the examined life as a whole or the interlocking narratives of MacIntyre, than the preoccupations of the secular citizen or collective, usually in the abstract. The stress in utilitarian philosophy on social consequences may give the impression of tying the individual to the whole, but it treats the former as an impersonal agent in the process of maximizing collective benefit. Again, the notion of a social contract to maximize justice for all treats the contracting parties as anonymous actors in a formula for shared existence, without asking who the actors are in imparting content and context to what they ought to do.

It may be countered that a liberal community of reason – consisting of individuals engaged in the communicative rationality of a modern civil society – does not require to be identified as anything more than citizens who are subject to public, rule-based morality. 'To know if someone is a "good" scientist,' it has been argued, 'it is not necessary to know anything about their "psychology" or moral make-up; it is necessary only to know if they are playing by the "rules of the game".'[23] To which one may couple a 'reflective equilibrium', where the individual mediates general rules for application to particular settings.[24] Is not the upshot the most practical ethics that we can summon with regard to individuals dealing with one another in pluralist communities? If so, then we might cogently have addressed *what* and *how* the individuals and communities at hand should take seriously as moral principles; but *why* they should do so? Self-interest alone cannot possibly account for why we should not only be altruistic, but also seek to do so to a prescribed standard. Moreover, do we really operate in a reflective equilibrium of cool rationality, dipping into a normative pool for answers to daily moral dilemmas in need of truthful solutions? Is a scientist who complies with a professional code of conduct thereby rendered 'good' rather than merely professional in his conduct? One defence of a liberalism that embraces an integrated view of individual and community argues that we are indeed ethically bound up in the social, insofar as (after Aristotle) life is a performance that ought to be done as well as possible, which requires us to recognize our communal rootedness.[25] Yet this, too, would make the code-compliant scientist 'good' in that he has performed well; it barely adds value beyond professionalism.

II

In his *Ethics and the Limits of Philosophy*, the Oxford philosopher Bernard Williams offered a sustained critique of how far removed modern moral theories were from grappling with the difficulty of how 'truthfulness to an existing self or society is to be combined with reflection, self-understanding, and criticism.'[26] While responding to this challenge might be helped by abstract reflection, the answers are ultimately to be found in 'reflective living', because ethical commitments only exist within the dispositions of actual individuals. That is, individuals are not mere ciphers for theoretical assignment of value or motivation; they have to be dealt with as actors faced with contextual choices, defining the 'good life' in their particular experience. There is no escaping the reality that it is the content of individual dispositions, their intelligibility and their degree of specificity, which differs among individuals, and among modern communities and societies.[27] More recently, Jürgen Habermas makes the same point in *The Future of Human Nature*, arguing that norms and insights 'bind the will only when they are embedded in an ethical self-understanding that joins the concern about one's own well-being with the interest in justice.'[28] The word 'bind' here should be taken in terms of motivating capacity, to which Habermas adverts,[29] not of 'obligation'. For the idea of reducing moral complexity to 'obligation' is precisely the sort of rule-based order that both he and, more explicitly, Williams, direct much of their critique.

Moral choices have to do with the 'deliberative priority' that is accorded to specific courses of action, and this priority in turn relates to a whole range of possible motivations, of which obligation is only one. Ethically outstanding choices may not be a matter of obligation at all, in that they cannot be demanded or the actor subjected to blame for not doing them; instead, they may be done because the actor feels there is no alternative for him personally, while recognizing that this could not be demanded of others.[30] Which brings us to shades of difference that often characterize contemporary usage of the terms 'ethics' and 'morals'. Sharing as they do Graeco-Latin roots (*ethikos, mores*, relating to 'custom'), they are often used interchangeably. In formal discourse, however, ethical perspectives are about what guides an individual or a community in choices that concern the 'good', relating closely to perceptions of who one is and how best to live in one's universe. Morals, on the other hand, are more specifically about rules that concern what is right or wrong, whether for the individual or society. Certainly the concepts overlap substantially in theory and practice; but it is well to bear in mind the more encompassing sense of reality that typifies ethics.[31]

Now this leads Habermas to infer that only in the domain of public morals can one ground 'rational solutions' to competing views
of what is right, in the shared interest of all. Ethical perspectives,
he says, are too tightly linked with identity-forming beliefs to allow
for such deliberation. Moral rules have the advantage of being able
to maintain neutrality vis-à-vis various worldviews, and thereby
support fundamental claims to human rights. Yet Habermas duly
recognizes that only through a suitable ethical orientation on the part
of individuals and communities will those rational moral solutions
be taken seriously, and not languish in an existential vacuum.[32] That
is, short of legislating or otherwise codifying such solutions, which
also speaks to the need to take the law seriously. It seems reasonable,
then, to conclude that it is within a pluralist ethos – true to its own
understanding of the self and the universe, but also committed to a
rational conception of the good – that moral claims, whether public
or private, must finally be embedded. That ethical views are connected
with identity-forming beliefs does not wed them, *ipso facto*, to a rigid
worldview. Unless, of course, one assumes that identities themselves
are inexorably set in time and space, in which instance their ethos
would be hard pressed to accommodate the moral and human rights
claims that stem from communicative rationality.

The question of whether a particular outlook corresponds to the
standard of a pluralist ethos with a commitment to deliberative morality is not about its religious or secular identity as such, but a matter
of actual as well as normative orientation. Just as there are secular
ideologies, including mainstream variants of Liberalism, that eschew
claims to the 'good' against what they perceive as 'just', so there are
religious outlooks that resist any departures from their orthodox conceptions of the good against fresh claims to justice. In positing that a
bona fide commitment to ethical conduct must involve the harmony
of external action and moral motivation, Nasir al-Din al-Tusi and
Kant in their different ways staked out an approach to mediating
the rational and the good. Both espoused Reason as central to their
moral venture, and nourished variant streams of humanist thought
and praxis, whether in religious or secular vein. Kant's 'categorical
imperative' and 'transcendental self' with a 'reverence for the law' may
seem at a considerable remove from al-Tusi's Intellect as the seat of

the Soul in a moral search for 'the perfection of defective faculties', until one recalls Kant's espousal of the ideal Church as an 'ethical republic' rejecting dogma in favour of 'rational faith'.[33] Still, Kant has properly been assailed for his excessively abstract deontology, and its heritage in Western philosophy,[34] against which al-Tusi epitomizes the notion of a 'lived ethics'.

The perspectives offered in the present study explore critical ethical themes in Muslim contexts today, mindful of scriptural, intellectual and cultural heritages and influences. As is already evident, non-Islamic currents run through those historic and contemporary elements, for reasons that have to do with the quintessentially shared nature of lived ethics. Indeed, the Qur'anic ethos itself embodies a plurality of cultural and confessional elements that Muslims made their own, a synthesis that would in its turn impact the metamorphosis of secular and religious frameworks far beyond the Muslim world. One often sees the characterization of modern Muslim discourse as involving conversations with authoritative scholars who lived long ago, alongside the need to 'return' to primary sources, in a 'quest for understanding of novel situations in light of traditional values.'[35] True enough – if this is not taken to imply that the ethical venture is effectively about 'applying' traditional norms to new problems. As already suggested, the understanding of those traditions as well as their content are themselves in constant flux, or should be in the name of a pluralist and rational stance that partakes fully of the modern. Even if 'life can only be understood backward,' Kierkegaard observed, 'it must be lived forward.'[36] An ethical critique of civic conduct, including of rigid, traditionalist applications of the Shari'a, remains characteristic of Muslim contexts (as shown elsewhere in this study) because it is supple in living forward. It entails conversations not only with interlocutors of the past, Muslim and otherwise, but also of the present. Among the most acute tests of its relevance, as well as fidelity, today are the emergent challenges posed by biomedical, ecological and development issues, in a techno-secular age with its peculiar theology and ethos.[37] The remainder of this essay focuses on some of the specific themes in that context that confront Muslims, as well as others, in ways old and new.

As evidence of a practical turn in Muslim ethico-philosophical discourse, one is inclined to cite the early derivation of juridical principles (*fiqh*) by communities whose rapid geo-cultural expansion beyond the original Arabian domain (*dar al-Islam*) mandated a rule of law that enjoyed the imprimatur of the new faith. Indeed, one may lament with Fazlur Rahman the overly legalistic guise that the Shari'a and *fiqh* conferred from the eighth to tenth centuries upon a discourse still in the early stages of metamorphosis as moral reasoning.[38] However, as the threads of this reasoning were picked up and woven into a full-fledged philosophical discourse by Miskawayh, al-Ghazali and al-Tusi, among others, it found rich application and maturation within the emergent sciences of Islam in the early medieval period. Medicine, in particular, as institutional-clinical practice and as a field of advanced learning, extended the normative *akhlaq* into the public sphere, building on a Hellenistic (as well as a significant Indian) legacy of pathology and its appropriate social locus. In founding the world's earliest hospitals (*bimaristan*) in Baghdad, Damascus and Cairo, while deploying the empirical method in a discipline hitherto dominated by theoretical modes of reasoning, Muslims and their Judaeo-Christian collaborators developed a humanistic ethos that prized the rational. It flourished across the urban centres of the Middle East – to cite Ahmad Dallal's seminal analysis – not only as part of Islam's civilizational impetus but also as a 'social institution'.[39]

Issues of professional conduct by health practitioners, open access to hospitals, and 'sensible' attitudes among patients, physicians and pharmacologists were of vital importance. In these matters, Hippocratic and Galenic writings were certainly influential. Yet here, as in the determination of those like 'Abd al-Latif al-Baghdadi (1162–1231) and Ibn al-Nafis (1213–88) to test canonical claims by rigorous anatomical samplings and examination,[40] Muslims made science and its universal outlook very much their own. A new medical ethics grew from the writings of 'Abbas al-Majusi (c. 925–94), Ibn al-Baytar (c.1190–1248), the Damascus medical school founder and teacher al-Dakhwar (d.1231), and his illustrious pupils Ibn Abi Usaybia (1194–1270) and Ibn al-Nafis himself, also a fine Hadith scholar.[41] In their writings, the practice of medicine – as art and science – acquired what might be described as a rational teleology:

it demanded the fullest commitment to pursuing scientific accuracy and truth, coupled with a recognition of the purposive nature of that pursuit as an extension of man's relationship with God. Virtually all the luminaries were trained not only in medicine but also in law and theology; sundered universes of secular science and religious morals did not exist. When al-Nafis was confronted with the *akhlaq* tenet that required the integrity of human organs to be preserved after death, he nonetheless found it justifiable to conduct cadaver dissections to establish vital facts (like the heart's ventricular structure) that made for effective treatment. Time and again, such rationales were found on behalf of therapeutic action and sound health.

While this may be interpreted as evincing the cognitive and value autonomy of science from 'Islam', it is more cogently seen in terms of an integrated ethos in which normative fidelities were balanced by a sense of the larger good.[42] It was here that the *akhlaq* values of compassion, charity, wisdom and solidarity found some of their most creative and conscious expression, beginning with the physician's Oath that put the welfare of the patient and the avoidance of harm at the forefront.[43] Nor is this in the least surprising: the encounters with birth, death and the elements that challenge them are, after all, the *métier* from which ethical narratives are derived and given meaning. The capacity of science in general, and medicine in particular, to account for – and control – key aspects of these fundamental encounters has long been obvious. Where that capacity is part of a broader canvas of shared meaning such as that provided by religion or other metaphysical sources, the ethical compass for action finally sits *outside* the scientific universe. One cannot offer a purely biological, chemical or other physical rationale in response to questions about the morality of an innovation or intervention. Al-Nafis could ground his defence of dissection and anatomical knowledge in *maslaha* (from *istislah*), the public good; he could not assert an absolute or unqualified right to pursue anatomical curiosity irrespective of the results.[44] With the advent of the techno-secular age, science often purports to provide its own ethical compass, rejecting social values that are deemed 'irrational'; yet motives of profit and publicity are part of the scientific warp and woof.

When the innovative and intervening prowess of medical science touches on the very foundations of birth, death and all that connects them, the relocation of the ethical compass matters all the more to society at large. 'We've discovered the secret of life!' gushed Francis Crick on 28 February 1953, after he and James Watson had established the three-dimensional structure of DNA that is the basis of cellular life. Their discovery made possible the Human Genome Project, which a half century later has decoded the sequence of the three billion DNA units in the human genome.[45] A leading proponent of that project, William Haseltine, is no less enthusiastic than was Crick about the implications for molecular biology: 'as we understand the body's repair process at the genetic level ... we will be able to advance the goal of maintaining our bodies in normal function, perhaps perpetually.'[46] The ability to fight through prevention and treatment a spectrum of disorders such as Alzheimer's and Parkinson's, cardiovascular disease and various forms of cancer would on its face seem a profoundly welcome outcome. But can those ends warrant the means involved in the process, such as gene intervention and manipulation whose effects we only dimly grasp, and which may radically alter the foundations of 'human nature'? Is there a stable human nature in the first instance whose alteration ought to raise moral concern? Where the ends include not simply preventing or treating disease but 'enhancing' the human body, biologically and aesthetically, where do we draw the line?

III

The answers can scarcely be sought within the confines of biotechnology itself, least of all for Muslim and other societies where techno-secular values do not have a putative primacy. Certainly, there is an overlap between the utilitarian and the religiously based ethic of maximizing public benefit from biomedical interventions – in Islam, on the basis of *maslaha* and *istihsan* (equity). But such claims must be tested against prior moral as well as human rights constraints regardless of the positive consequences, and mindful of the risks involved. Nor can one ignore commercial factors that have ramifications for how seriously we take claims to serving the public good or pursuing 'pure' science. The stakes on hand make the exercise of nuanced moral reasoning more intricate than ever, between the application of given norms on the one hand and of professional standards on the other. If the former runs the hazard of retreating into a traditionalism that is divorced from modern imperatives, then the secular extreme can spur reliance on 'situational' reasoning where *ad hocery* prevails, or on regulatory schemes that are impelled by ideological or corporate concerns.[47] The problem is illuminated when one considers the standard bioethical guidelines that have come to be adopted by clinicians in the West, viz. the 'four principles' of beneficence, nonmaleficence, autonomy and justice.[48] 'Do no harm' (nonmaleficence or *darar* in Arabic) as a rule of professional conduct may be well grounded universally as a starting point for the clinician; but determining what constitutes 'harm' and how to resolve conflicts between the principles themselves (such as when the wishes of the patient clash with the obligations of the clinician) requires a degree of specificity that clearly takes us outside the realm of biomedicine itself.

The public policy dilemma in balancing secular and faith-based perspectives in this matter is summed up by a veteran Catholic US Congressman thus: 'When principles are at issue, they [the bishops] simply look them up. Too many liberals, alas, simply make them up.'[49] For Muslims, steering an accountable course on issues ranging from cloning and organ transplants to abortion and euthanasia occurs within an ethos that integrates *din* (religious) and *duniya* (secular), while recognizing their separate institutional domains.[50] That ethos is pluralist, in keeping not only with varying doctrinal views but also the flux of historical and cultural context and the emergence of human rights norms. Here are some examples that illuminate the specific dilemmas that stem from today's biomedical and social realities.

Abortion

Induced as opposed to involuntary termination of pregnancy (*ijhad* or *saqt*) has long been the subject of ethico-legal analysis among Muslims,[51] attracting a broad range of stances on questions of doctrine and public policy. Involuntary abortion or miscarriage is usually regarded as 'natural' and bears no moral sanction – unless it stems from negligence, which carries its own burden. Induced abortion engages a host of ethical themes that relate to timing and circumstance, which also underpin the various *fiqh* or legal stances thereon. On the basis of Qur'anic verses that refer to the development of the foetus from zygote and embryo to 'another creature' (22:5, 23:14), ensoulment of the foetus is generally thought to occur 120 days from conception (a minority regards the operative period to be 40 days).[52] This is distinct from the question 'when does life begin?' in biological terms.[53] However, the ensoulment phase is widely thought to be the pertinent boundary for a voluntary abortion on approved grounds; safeguarding the mother's health is the traditionally approved basis. As contraceptive devices gained approval across the Muslim world from the 1950s onward, drawing in part on the traditional acceptance of *coitus interruptus* ('azl), modern opinion has often treated abortion within the 120-day phase as legitimate birth control.[54] The Shi'a tradition in general is especially permissive in this respect. Other scholars have argued that 'azl is not a proper analogy because an embryo/foetus is an 'existing presence' (*mawjud hasil*), a perspective that goes back to al-Ghazali.

What we have, then, are plural ethical approaches and not simply competing doctrinal views on the specific issues. One approach stresses the pragmatic results that are considered desirable, notably family planning and protecting the mother, which are considered to outweigh the undesirability of ending a potential life. Another deems abortion to be inherently disapproved, subject only to protecting the mother; the social context is not considered relevant. Yet the choice of approach in legal regulation and ethics, public and private, does not occur in a social vacuum. There is increasingly ready access to non-surgical forms of abortion like the 'morning-after' and 'RU486' pills, as well as to clinical sites of varying degrees of safety for abortion, often beyond the ambit of local or national frontiers. New medical understandings of foetal development, changing demographic and economic climates in a society, together with the impact of media portrayals of alternative lifeworlds (whether negative or positive), provide the practical canvas against which both public and individual interpretations of ethico-legal norms take place. Between a woman's human right to basic autonomy on the one hand, and the protection of a foetus's claim to life on the other, coercive legal regulation may be of limited effect or efficacy. Rather, a choice of what the bioethicist Margaret Somerville calls 'competing sorrows' becomes the dominant personal and societal moral reality.[55]

Human genetic intervention

The prevailing global public debate on aspects of cell cloning (*instinsakh*) in humans as well as animals gained urgency in 1997 with the birth of Dolly the sheep in Scotland, the first mammal to be cloned from the frozen cells of another.[56] She was the identical twin of a long-dead adult, and gave birth to six lambs, before dying in 2003 after suffering from acute arthritis and a lung infection.[57] 'This experiment made people think very differently about biology,' noted Dolly's cloner, Ian Wilmut, making us 'much more ambitious and optimistic' about stem cells as replacement cells for human beings.[58] Stem cells, present in small numbers in most organs, are significant because they have the 'plasticity' to develop into virtually any kind of tissue – especially if they come from embryos, rather than adults whose cells are currently thought to have less plasticity.[59] Those stem cells may be taken from existing embryos or derived from a process of fusing a cell and an egg whose nucleus has been removed.[60] Where cloning is used to foster cell lines that may help create tissues and organs, it is labelled 'therapeutic'; alternatively, the embryo derived from the fusion of cell and egg may be implanted in a uterus for reproductive cloning, as with Dolly the sheep. Reproductive cloning is at this juncture only successful with great difficulty in mammals,[61] and while there are scientists as well as others who do not find it morally objectionable, most people appear to do so. It is becoming the subject of tight regulation under national as well as international laws.[62]

By contrast, a qualified ethical acceptance of therapeutic cloning of stem cells appears to have emerged, not least in the Muslim world with its comparatively permissive stance on early embryonic status. A new stem cell research centre in Saudi Arabia, for example, will have the endorsement of *fatwas* that emphasize the public welfare element (*maslaha*) in allowing the use of cells taken from miscarried or aborted foetuses, subject to the 120-day norm.[63] However, there are potential grounds for ethical concern about therapeutic cloning, which in practice straddles 'therapy' and 'enhancement'. Stem cells developed for muscle tissue, for instance, may assist therapy for cardiac damage or muscular dystrophy, yet the same process could lend itself for commercial use in boosting muscular or cardiac tissue for elite sportsmen.[64] It is doubtful that *maslaha* could justify the second choice as a rationale for cloning. A related issue is that of equitable access to biomedical resources within and among societies, if there is not to be a 'biotech divide' in favour of the privileged few.[65] Then there is the prospect that embryos created by the same process of fusion for therapeutic cloning may end-up being implanted for reproductive purposes, either by accident or by design to circumvent legal constraints. At a more fundamental level, one must ask whether genetic manipulation and control may impact the autonomous basis of the identity of humans as responsible for their fate, and as ends in themselves rather than as instruments for ends chosen by others.[66] Could we in the process put at risk the gamut of human responses that allows us to connect with other human beings as individuals and communities?[67] As Muslim health professionals and scholars reflect on these questions,[68] the rush of developments in the laboratory and biotechnological market only elevates the ante.

Euthanasia

While the ethics of genetic intervention and abortion begin with the primacy of the life's sanctity in Islam, and then may venture into qualifying factors of the public welfare that shape the final response to the specific issue, euthanasia as an *active* act of 'mercy killing' (literally 'good death') is approached in more absolute terms. For it is treated as suicide on the part of the individual, with no reprieve on grounds of medical necessity.[69] Typically, *The Islamic Code of Medical Ethics* (Appendix C below) holds that a physician 'shall not take away life even when motivated by mercy,' basing itself on Prophetic guidance against suicide.[70] In the face of pain, the philosophical response is fortitude (*sabr*) borne of the conviction that the body is not one's property to dispose of but a custodial charge; the medical response is expected to be pain alleviation.[71] Where a medical condition reduces the body to a vegetative state or medical intervention is otherwise deemed futile, the same principle of sanctity/dignity allows for treatment to cease and life to lapse. Or, as the *Islamic Code* casts it, the physician must then recognize his limits as upholder of life, and may desist from 'heroic measures' or other passive preservation of the patient. However, active euthanasia – such as by lethal injection – remains prohibited in all circumstances. The broad (and sometimes difficult) distinction between passive and active euthanasia in Western medical ethics[72] is not, therefore, irrelevant in a Muslim context.[73] But though the patient's right to demand the cessation of treatment *in extremis*, along with 'informed consent' to such cessation vis-à-vis the caregivers, has a central place in Western bioethics, it does not appear to command the same attention in the *Islamic Code* at present; the explanation may be that the traditional norms against suicide and the body as a custodial charge prevail.[74] Yet, one is cognisant of gaps between precept and practice on this score, especially in light of the universalization of medical practice standards.[75]

Those ethically opposed to active euthanasia in contemporary Western discourse have invoked arguments that resonate with the Muslim stances outlined. Factors such as an intense individualism that finds expression in a body-as-property perspective, coupled with a decline in community support for dying individuals who face institutional loneliness, are felt to impel the trend in demanding the legalization of euthanasia. Further, 'new genetic and reproductive technologies have given us a sense that we understand and may manipulate the origin and nature of human life,' which applied 'to the other end of life makes euthanasia seem acceptable.'[76] Indeed, these considerations may in time weigh on Muslim societies as part of the advent of techno-social modernity. After all, it is precisely the advances in medical care, institutional development and socio-economic freedom that have fed demands for legalized euthanasia in North America and Western Europe.[77] Might the physician's obligation under the *Islamic Code* to safeguard 'freedom from pain and misery' on the part of the individual patient then acquire a greater profile? At the same time, given the risk entailed in physician-assisted suicide, which remains beyond the pale in most jurisdictions across the world (both because of the scope for abuse and the need to preserve the physician's normative commitment to the sanctity of life), society must remain alert to its stake in the wider context in which individual autonomy in ending life is asserted.

Organ donation and transplant

The potency of scriptural advocacy to 'bid the good' (*yamuruna bi-l maruf*) is captured in the decree by Islam's second caliph, 'Umar ibn Khattab (634–44 CE), that responsibility for a man who died of hunger was shared by his community, which was obligated to pay ransom (*fidya*) as if they had in fact killed him. This has prompted a modern analogy to derive an obligation on the part of those with the appropriate capacity to engage in donating blood and organs such as kidneys. 'Obligations' of this kind on behalf of society at large, *fardh kifaya* (contrasted with *fardh 'ayn*, obligations that rest on every individual distinctively), are regarded as a vital element in the ethos of the *umma* as a civic community.[78] In this context, it is bolstered by the norm in Prophetic guidance that the saving of life warrants all essential measures, including transgressions of standard prohibitions – 'even if it requires transplants from the dead.'[79] These evocations are commonly offered not only to urge an affirmative civility in response to chronic shortages in supplies of blood and human organs, but also to overcome normative counter-weights. For the hallowed notion of 'bodily integrity' raises for some the issue of desecrating the body by severing its parts – which in the past has even caused resistance to postmortem examinations (discussed earlier).[80] Likewise, the tenet that the body is a custodial charge rather than individual property might be read to imply that organ donations, in life or death, are violations of sacred trust. Those objections are put in perspective by recalling the far greater dignity and obligation in serving the collective good.[81] At the same time, however, the custodial nature of body 'ownership' is deemed to preclude the sale of organs, in conjunction with protecting society's more vulnerable members from commercial exploitation.

More vexing ethically are recent developments relating to organs taken from animals (xenotransplants) and their genetic modification for this purpose (transgenic breeding). Crossing the species barrier for body parts is not, in itself, a medical novelty. Bones from animals were famously used to heal human fractures in Muhammad's time, for example, and Muslim physicians also reportedly used animal bones to make dentures. However, xenotransplants of complex organs are a relatively modern phenomenon,[82] and the use of the pig as the commonest source of organs has obvious sensitivity. It is readily argued that if necessity justifies Muslims consuming the flesh of swine, then it certainly warrants transplants.[83] Pigs and other animals that are 'farmed' as organ sources for humans raise problems in two important respects.[84] First, their confinement in special conditions to preserve them from infections tends to be highly oppressive; mindful of the imperatives on the treatment of non-human animals in Muslim and other frameworks,[85] the avoidance of harm must occupy a conspicuous place in the assertion of 'ethical necessity'. Second, in order to mute human biological rejection of alien organs (especially acute for xenotransplants), the genomes of source animals are modified, often by inserting human genes. Cloning is undertaken to preserve a supply of transgenic animals. The perils in the mixing of genomes can't be taken lightly, as shown by recent global experience with contagion;[86] the social and ethical implications of proceeding with new biotechnologies in this area have led to regulatory restraints in several countries. Still, it would compound matters if a decline in public trust led to apprehension about organ donations – and about more benign biotechnologies – especially in communities where these need to be robustly cultivated to sustain the heritage of a positive communal ethos.

IV

A plethora of other bioethical concerns could be added to the foregoing, from sex-selection, surrogate motherhood and geriatric end-of-life situations to the cultivation of genetically modified foods – together with broader socio-ethical issues such as same-sex relationships and unions. Suffice it for our purposes to observe that the ethics of each issue tends in Muslim, as in religious and indeed secular contexts, to be approached from contending analytical angles. One inquires into the inherent rightness or wrongness, 'red lines' that ought not to be crossed at all – or crossed only on grounds deemed compelling enough. Another prefers to inquire whether the foresee-able consequences of an action (or inaction, as in 'passive' euthanasia) are morally desirable for the actor and the larger community. The former concerns the acuity of our moral intuitions; the latter requires a more deliberate rationality. Neither is dispensable for a lived ethics. Even though the answers they offer may appear sharply divergent, they ultimately must work in tandem. It may be decided, for example, that therapeutic cloning for the purpose of treating Alzheimer's disease is acceptable on the basis of the consequentialist approach. This would not dispense with the prospect of 'red lines' within and beyond the scope of the action: whose cells are being cloned and what conditions are regarded as 'acceptable' in the process (such as in the manipulation of animal genes)? What would be the implications of the research apropos of gene therapies, including intervention at the foetal or neonatal stage where the propensity for Alzheimer's is considered high? The unforeseeable risks in seemingly benign inter-vention, and the *bio-determinism* that rears its head, call for intuitive acuity to be kept very much alive. Ironically, the implicit loss in hu-man autonomy, along with the more general lapse into resignation about the capacity of genes/DNA to determine human behaviour, emanates from our 'rational' impulses, scientific and otherwise.[87]

But there is a further sense in which intuitive capacities are crucial for practical ethics, beyond the red line and consequentialist ways of looking at issues. Let us suppose that Soraya, a healthy woman, donates one of her kidneys to her brother, Nadim. After a successful transplant, she visits him in the hospital where Nadim expresses his deep gratitude to her. Soraya responds that she could have done no less in the circumstances: the hospital advised that the transplant was essential and likely to be successful, that she was the most suitable do-nor and the risk to her was small. Accordingly, she felt it was her duty to donate. We may understand this to be rational and responsible, and would likely regard a failure to donate by Soraya as morally culpable (barring other compelling reasons). She can be said to have fulfilled the Kantian critique that only an act motivated by an undiluted sense of duty counts morally – or the utilitarian one that society should be able to count on siblings delivering on mutual obligations in order to relieve the usual pressures on the health system for matching organs.

Yet neither evaluation seems entirely satisfactory. Is Nadim not entitled to expect that Soraya's motivation ought to go beyond duty, to acting foremost out of affection ? The gap between doing 'right' and doing 'good' is evident.[88] Matters of affection and personal commitment are not marginal but key facets of the context – the *telos* or whole life – in which moral choices find meaning.[89] There is more to those choices than obligations, and more to the *telos* than choices. It may be that Soraya's sense of duty sprang from a disposition tied to affection and the good; if so, then the 'bottom-line' was not obligation. For this is the domain of character, where intuitions are rife in shaping one's views and conduct in the real world. It is also where religions stake their claim on the human conscience not just at the point where one encounters a difficult choice, but in the continuum of mind and routine habit.

From Aquinas's adaptation of Aristotle's natural law into Christian teachings to Gandhi's instilling of *satyagraha* (truth and firmness), to Zen Buddhism today, character is the locus of the good. For Muslims, this certainly finds expression on the metaphysical plane, as in Ibn 'Arabi's doctrine of *wahdat al-wujud* or 'unity of being' in which the virtues are lived.[90] But Islam, as already noted, is wedded quintessentially to character-in-action, wherein the *umma* serves as the vehicle for practical ethics. The Caliph 'Umar's decree that a society shared the burden for the fate of its hungry members expressed a civic ethos, while a plurality of *tariqas* came to embody solidarities of the spirit in personal as well as institutional action.[91] The *telos* framing the acts or virtues of the individual and the community gives a central place to the notion of custodianship in Islam at several levels: the community as caretaker for its members, especially the disadvantaged (those disabled or indigent, orphaned or widowed); the individual as fiduciary for those in his/her charge; the human body itself as a charge on behalf of the Maker.

Underlying these is the Qur'anic bestowal of trust (*amana*) and vicegerency (*khilafa*) upon humankind with regard to the earth (33: 72, 35:39), for which the 'inheritors' have the fullest accountability. This is no fall from grace into nature, as in Aquinas, but a quest within what Nomanul Haq calls a 'cosmology of justice' that links our *telos* to ecological ethics:

It ought to be recognized that the Qur'an does contain verses that *prima facie* give the impression that the natural world and all its creatures exist for the sake of human beings, but it would be a gross oversimplification to view such declarations in a moral vacuum. 'In considering all these verses,' wrote the outstanding jurist ... Ibn Taymiyya (d. 1328), 'it must be remembered that God in His wisdom brought into being these creatures for reasons other than serving human beings. In these verses God only explains the [human] benefits of these.' ... Islam does not have to carry the burden of any scriptural imperative to 'subdue' the earth and seek to establish 'dominion' over the natural world. There is a clear and explicit answer to the question as to where and to whom belongs the dominion over the natural world, an answer so obvious in the overall drift of the Qur'an that it is expressed rhetorically: 'Knowest thou not that to God belongeth the dominion of the heavens and the earth?'[92]

An extensive body of socio-economic and legal literature as well as practice has built on this foundation, touching on issues such as fair access to water, the husbanding of flora, fauna and soils, the proper treatment of animal life, and the aesthetics of public gardens. The notion of *hima* (protected space) evolved from scripture and Hadith into an instrument of policy to create sanctuaries for forests, grazing and related environmental purposes in the public interest – parallel to the *haram* (sacred space), which extended beyond places of worship to natural springs and wells, vulnerable plants and wastelands.[93] Privileged status is accorded to gardens (*bustan*, *bagh*) as appendages to mosques, tombs and palaces as well as independent public refuges, celebrated from Moorish Spain to Mughal India as earthly reflections of Paradise. These are not only symbolic or functional elements but entail recognition of intrinsic merit within the schema of natural balance and its counterpart in social justice.[94] Hence the solemn rituals that must attend the licit slaughter of animals (*dhabh*) – and the injunctions that abound on their humane treatment. The Prophetic tradition, 'Do not treat the back of your animals as pulpits, God the Most High has made them subject to you only to convey you to a place which you could not otherwise reach without much difficulty,' is exemplary; cats, sparrows, dogs and livestock feature in innumerable exhortations, leading to the *fiqh* rule making animal owners liable for their well-being.[95] Muhammad's acute distress at seeing the branding of an animal's face and at the idea of blood sports finds its way into the normative corpus.[96]

Stewardship ethics today pervades the discourse on the environment and sustainable development,[97] against the wider background of globalization and its decidedly mixed implications for both.[98] Secular and religious ways of approaching 'stewardship' differ particularly when it comes to normative views of dominion over nature in Judaeo-Christian traditions;[99] but the emphasis on accountable trust in Muslim ethics narrows the discrepancy considerably. It is rewarding on this score to consider the approach in the operational framework of the Aga Khan Development Network (AKDN), which aims to 'realise the social conscience of Islam through institutional action' (*Ethical Framework*, Appendix B). Engaged across the Muslim and developing worlds in cooperation with national and global agencies as well as civil society,[100] its ethos of sustainable environment and governance lays special emphasis on resource management in conditions of 'trust, probity, equity and accountability', mindful of the need to preserve ecological balances. Certainly, dealing with legacies ranging from poor nuclear waste disposal to mega-projects with repercussions for the human and physical environment is as much a challenge in 'Muslim' as other contexts. A recent independent appraisal of AKDN projects in Tajikistan singles out the commitment to local consultation and ownership as well as to long-term self-sustainability of projects as key markers of its success.[101] While the 'Ethical Framework' draws specific inspiration from the Shi'i Muslim tradition, this prompts an inclusive view of 'communities and nations ... to harness individual and group differences and talents,' including sensitivity to gender equity. A routine test of this occurs in a multiplicity of programme locales, from South Asia to the Near East and sub-Saharan Africa, where the socio-cultural diversity of the beneficiaries is evident.

These commitments to ecological stewardship – and their parallels with respect to biomedical, corporate and other public practices – call attention to the nexus between ethical and legal orientation. Since tangible sanctions usually attach to the law as compared with the more voluntary nature of ethical codes, the willingness to legalize or otherwise make enforceable such commitments often becomes the criterion of 'seriousness'. This seems especially reasonable in the regulatory realm where effective protection of the public interest has primacy; equally, an appeal to that interest at the moral level is of obvious import for the law itself. Legislation to foster urban green spaces, or to ensure thresholds in the treatment of captive animals or the use of embryonic stem cells, relies on shared values beyond deference to the rule of law – hence, the assumption that the law reflects a society's ethos, signalling the obligations deemed most fundamental.[102] Yet, the profuse legalization of the public sphere can obscure the vitality of ethical life in its own right, as will be seen apropos of themes relating to civic culture and pluralism in the essays that follow. This essay has embraced the view that obligations provide an inadequate explanation of the intricacy of ethical life on the personal plane. That is no less true of societal issues where there is more to taking public virtues seriously than legislating them. Obligations may impart a sense of legitimate expectation and reliability, but they fail to capture the *telos* where choices and character converge.

For Muslims, the overlap of individual and public interest – indeed, of the individual as an extension not only of the *umma* but also a cosmic *telos* – is part of the principle of *ulm al-nafs*, of wrong to the other as injury to the self.[103] As such, it lends a poignancy all its own to Kierkegaard's observation quoted at the outset, on the individual as life-editor who answers to the order of things in which he lives, and thereby to God. It does no less, surely, for the commitment that Abdolkarim Soroush calls for to the concrete and accessible in taking ethics seriously.

Chapter 2

Civility and its Discontents

I

Mainstream liberal discourse on civic culture has accorded a less than conspicuous place to substantive ethical tenets amid the ascendancy of rights and the rule of law in the public square. To be sure, codes of conduct for public actors such as physicians, lawyers, teachers, financial officers and even politicians abound – oriented generally to professional propriety rather than to conceptions of the 'good'. But the secular mind has come to mistrust public and collective virtues as coercive and ideological, which find expression in talk of the Good Society – not of Civil Society, the favoured path to enhancement of democratic values and practice.[1] Of late, with the emergence of vexing biomedical, ecological and social issues (discussed in the preceding essay), the rights-centred framing of public debates has begun to encounter serious challenge. Nevertheless, the assumption holds that the proper basis for a modern civic culture, of universal application, involves the pursuit of a secular civil divested of private virtue. Applied to the transitional societies of the Muslim world, this paradigm is seen to run into profound, if not *sui generis*, barriers of history, ideology and religion. In particular, Islam's supposed merging of the categories of secular, sacred and state (*duniya, din, dawla*), as well as the concept of *umma* as a transcendent community, are seen as inherently problematic for an inclusive, pluralist and secular ethos where one freely associates with others outside the control of the state.

If impetus were required for fresh thinking on what is at stake in this regard on the part of Muslims themselves and the liberal West, it has been furnished by the events of September 11, 2001, and their aftermath.[2] The public arena on every continent has since been convulsed in debate over the implications for 'Islamic' political culture. Admittedly, the ensuing debate has all too frequently degenerated into polemics that stoke cultural prejudice and often wilfully deny the socio-economic and political roots of 'religious extremism', in which the West is often complicit.[3] But that cannot be allowed to detract from the pressing need to examine the role of ethical values in the public culture of the Muslim world, notably with regard to accountability to the citizenry in all its diversity, and the issue of political violence in the context of civility. For ethical affinities at the personal and communal levels alike remain a hallmark of Muslim conceptions of social being.

Historically, this perspective can be traced to the founding tenets of the Prophet Muhammad's Medina, through the celebrated works of al-Farabi and Ibn Rushd, and down to modern conceptions of the ideal polity.[4] Can such a perspective be reconciled with the modern conception of the public sphere, the secular civic space that is considered essential to civil society?[5] Or should that quest be undertaken on its own terms, and the ethical affinities of old consigned by and large to the private sphere? Is it not sufficient to ground issues of accountability, pluralism and nonviolence in a secular ethos of human rights? There are compelling reasons, in my view, for embracing the ethical option, even if it entails a reconception of the nature of the public sphere in light of indigenous Muslim experiences.

I sketch here first what appear to be the salient contours of the liberal discourse that leads to a dichotomy between norms of 'civic' and 'ethical' conduct, as an integral part of the privileging of secular, individual rights. One recalls the original Roman idea of citizenship embodied in participation in the *civitas* or public square, now extended to the democratic modern polity with an ethos of civility. 'Civility' captures the virtue of commitment to the whole of the *civitas*, the poles of friends and foes alike.[6] A Muslim critique is applied here to this continually unfolding discourse – before both are finally brought to bear on social and political realities in the Muslim world. I hasten to add that at this juncture, the nature of the analysis is necessarily preliminary and certainly does not purport do justice to every facet of the complex discursive relationships on hand (including the socio-economic implications of globalization, and of new biomedical technologies). An exhaustive critique awaits manifold contributions – Muslim as well as non-Muslim – across disciplinary lines, and drawing upon a more extensive body of sociological data than is available at this time.

For contemporary liberalism, a minimal consensus on moral and ethical precepts[7] is part of the *quid pro quo* for a maximal consensus on the rules and mores of coexistence amid diversity. 'The ethic central to a liberal society is an ethic of the right rather than the good,' Charles Taylor has observed; hence, 'its basic principles concern how society should respond to arbitrate the competing demands of individuals.'[8] In consequence and effect, 'society must be neutral on the question of the good life,' that is, on what most of us would deem the core question of personal and social ethics.[9] Indeed, even the classical, Aristotelian definition of the 'good' in ethical context arguably amounted to just such a perspective in its pragmatic stress on what is appropriate (rather than morally correct), from a situational as well as personal stance.[10] Again, the powerful impulse to the emergence of modern civil society imparted by the Scottish Enlightenment also celebrated virtue – but as 'private mores rather than public commitments'.[11] The individuated self trumped the social in a trend that also became the hallmark of Anglo-American jurisprudence. At its most emphatic, this has culminated in what Richard Rorty considers a compromise of higher amorality: the many, competing quests for Truth have all been discredited anyway, so democratic pragmatism favours moral indifference.[12]

Another way of framing this central liberal 'bargain', in terms closer to the conceptual and policy concerns of civil society, is that the more a state is committed to a minimal agenda of upholding negative liberties (that is, freedoms from abusive intrusions against the sanctity of the individual and his choices), the greater the prospect of maximizing the plural goals that citizens and communities wish to pursue – and the less the danger of utopian engineering of the kind required in pursuit of particular virtues or ideologies that forestall the openness of civic culture. It is no surprise that this perspective, which is associated with the writings of Isaiah Berlin and Karl Popper,[13] emerged from the mid–20th century European experience that culminated in key international human rights agreements.[14] Nor that it should have found deep resonance in post-cold war eastern and central Europe where the current discourse on civil society experienced its strongest rebirth, through the writings (and activism) of Vaclav Havel, John Keane, Ernest Gellner, George Soros and others.[15] In both of those European contexts, nothing could be perceived as more threatening to the vibrancy of civic culture than ideology emanating from an authoritarian state, the church or fascist social movements.

II

Much of liberal discourse seeks to privatize ethics and morality, or at least the moral dimension of ethics. There can hardly be a total severing of ties between the tenets of social ethics and those of civic culture, given the shared preoccupation with upholding 'appropriate' behaviour (in regard to public order, accountable governance and participatory politics, the integrity of the environment and other fundamental values). However, ethics *qua* judgments about 'good' conduct are, as noted, generally outside the parameters of the public sphere. Indeed for some, such judgments fall outside the realm of ethics itself, seen increasingly as being about 'practical virtues' like accountability and transparency. In the most widely discussed recent work on civic culture in Western perspective, Robert Putnam's *Bowling Alone*,[16] there is not a single direct reference to ethics in the former substantive sense. Putnam, whose 1996 essay of the same title triggered an enormous academic and policy debate, makes reference to altruism, philanthropy, trust and honesty as well as religious participation.[17] But nowhere are ethics deemed worthy of consideration in their own right as a vital facet of the public sphere where civic engagement happens.

Still more recently, John Ralston Saul, a leading Canadian public intellectual, has argued that neither public nor private ethics should be 'confused with morality', since 'ethics is not about good intentions.'[18] Saul is right to warn that moral certainty can quickly transmute into political evil. But if the road to Hell is paved with good intentions, can an amoral ethics get us to Heaven? The answer on the other side of the Atlantic, in Joan Smith's *Moralities,*[19] appears to be in the affirmative. She assails the notion that social ethics can embrace judgments about right and wrong without encountering a fatal skepticism. For Smith, Judaeo-Christian ethics have been discredited by the behaviour (and 'Victorian' sensibilities) of proponents who have fed a hypocritical disjuncture between precept and practice.[20] Hence, public morality rests in the more pluralist culture of human rights.[21]

Given that a secular landscape is felt to be the proper locus for modern civic culture,[22] perhaps this rejection is predictable, though certainly not inevitable. A robust occidental critique of that liberal posture has emerged in the past decade, spearheaded by the 'communitarian movement' that draws upon liberal values like the rule of law and pluralism, coupled with the civic republican tenets of social trust, self-help and community-building. Among the leading trans-Atlantic proponents of communitarianism are Amitai Etzioni, Anthony Giddens, John Gray, Gertrude Himmelfarb, Robert Kuttner, Robert Putnam and Michael Sandel. They are a broad church with varying political affiliations but joined by their primary concern about the corrosive effects of liberal individualism on civic solidarity and engaged citizenship.[23] For Himmelfarb and others on the more conservative end of the communitarian spectrum, the traditional morality dismissed by Smith is a condition *sine qua non* to advance civil society; any other brand of 'social ethics' simply lacks substance and undermines the desired civic ethos. For Giddens, Kuttner and other more liberal communitarians, it is chiefly economic/free market individualism that undercuts social solidarity. To counter this tendency, public policy must draw upon a shared ethos of civic patriotism. Both conservative and liberal tendencies appear to decry the sharp dichotomy between private and public ethics that is the staple of mainstream liberalism and its conception of civil society.

Yet the communitarian critique has also been seized upon by those with a less pluralist commitment, and pressed into the service of a cultural patriotism that privileges a particular view of the Judaeo-Christian ethic. In the influential writings of Samuel P. Huntington on the 'clash of civilizations', for example, what is seen as a decline in fealty to traditional values (including respect for education, family integrity and the rule of law) is treated as a root cause of growing Euro-American political and economic weakness in relation to other cultural zones or civilizations, most notably that of Islam.[24] As I have noted elsewhere, Huntington sees no contradiction in issuing a summons on behalf of 'Western' ethical values that pointedly degrades the multicultural components (and citizenry) of Euro-American polities.[25] At the same time, he is oblivious of the new realities of global citizenship and culture that enlarge civic membership beyond traditional frontiers of nationality and geography. Huntington's thesis also lends itself to a validation of a closed view of society in response to the incursion of non-Western values and people[26] – which would, one is inclined to think, be antithetical to the open society envisaged by most theorists as vital to a mature civic culture.

The communitarian movement and other critiques of the 'radical secularity' (after Taylor) of occidental civil society tend to find themselves defending, at best, a marginal nexus between morally-based social ethics and the modern public sphere. In this vein, Etzioni asserts that the moral revivalists among his fellow communitarians are really in pursuit of the Good Society rather than Civil Society,[27] implying that social virtues need to be siphoned-off from civic values.[28] Inasmuch as the rationale here is a concern for civil liberties and the rule of law (as opposed to the emphasis on individual responsibilities by moral revivalists), it seems to reaffirm the primacy of an individualist ethos in the civic calculus.[29] It also brings us full circle to Gellner's stance that modern man must choose between being 'modular' – that is, 'individualist and egalitarian, while nevertheless capable of cohesion against the state'[30] – or being 'communalist' in his resistance to bonds outside of kinship, religion and tribe.[31] This captures the essence of a liberal definition of civil society that is mistrustful of serious ethical affinities. The corollary for Muslim and other 'segmentary' communities, as Gellner sees it, is a choice between the traditional bonds of the *umma* and the strictly secular bonds of pluralist civic modernity.[32]

There is plenty that Gellner and other mainstream theorists can be challenged about in the sweeping assumptions about Islam, the *umma* and what constitutes 'civic culture'.[33] Apart from the Orientalist overtones of some of those assumptions, the notion that the social capital generated by communal bonds is vitiated by a uniform resistance to freely moving in and out of such associations is surely anchored in a limited understanding of how fluid those bonds often are – as Dale Eickelman, John Esposito and others have documented.[34] One recalls, too, the paradigm of 'discourse ethics' as a vital aspect of the ideal public sphere that has been sketched by Jürgen Habermas.[35] Our paramount concern here, however, is specifically with the unfolding nexus between social ethics and civil society in mainstream liberal and, in the rest of this analysis, transitional Muslim contexts. I say 'transitional' in recognition of the quest for democratic modernity and its attendant civic culture that marks the contemporary reality of those societies and communities, whether or not this is shared by the governments of the day. Muslim intellectual and activist critiques – unlike those of their Western counterparts – are directed less at existing indigenous 'models' than at putative/emerging ones, even if they are acutely mindful of particular approaches (like the opposing ones of Iran and Turkey). The stakes range far beyond mere theory, to the realm of competing choices with far-reaching social and political implications.

III

Before venturing into the rationales for an ethically-oriented Muslim approach to civic culture, it is necessary to delineate the elements that define the latter outside the bounds of liberal, conservative or other political ideology. Most theorists and activists would concur that any modern conception of civil society must include three requisite elements: the rule of law, equal citizenship and participatory politics with state accountability to the civic sphere. These primary elements in turn favour the organic separation of state and society, the independence of the judiciary as well as of the media, and guarantees of free association and thought. Only then is it meaningful to invoke a public sphere in which civic interaction can occur. Yet, no matter

how desirable the existence of this civic culture in a secure and legitimate public space, it is value-neutral in the sense of commanding
no allegiance to specific moral principles. There are certainly moral
dimensions to human rights that uphold the integrity of individual
and communal life, belief and equality; but appeals to secular law are
sufficient to safeguard these entitlements.

The value-neutral nature of these elements also accounts for how
a rigorous critic of liberal ideology like E.P. Thompson could be ef-
fusive about an institution often associated with economic and social
inequity: 'the rule of law itself, the imposing of effective inhibitions
upon power and the defence of the citizen from power's all-intrusive
claims, seems to me to be an unqualified human good.'[36] Thompson's
recognition of the *instrumental* value of the rule of law in limiting state
power and safeguarding individual liberties had nothing to do with
ethical or moral value; his praise could be rephrased as 'an unqualified civic good.' Likewise, writing of the revival of the rule of law as a
cornerstone of democratic transitions since the end of the Cold War,
Thomas Carothers singles out as its defining traits public knowledge,
transparency and equal application to all, including the government.[37]
While those traits may be seen as necessary conditions for a liberal
ethos, Carothers notes their embrace across ideological lines.

The same is true of the other defining elements above, from equal
citizenship to the freedom of worship: each is cherished instrumen-
tally *qua* civic good in this 'procedural liberal' perspective. Indeed,
the logic extends to the institutional basis of secular culture – the
separation of church and state – that accompanies the autonomy of
state and civic spheres in civil society. True, there is much to contest
even in a nuanced appreciation of what secularism means. But secular
culture as an institutional facet of civil society is here taken to be
value-neutral, without the anti-religious resonance that often attaches
to it in other contexts.[38]

The liberal characterization of civil society as – ideally – a zone of
freedom, tolerance and politico-economic choice that can face down
the despotism of states and even the atomization of communities,[39]
clearly stems from very specific experience. This includes historical
contests among monarchical and church institutions and the emerging bourgeoisie, and the more recent east/central European tussles

between totalitarian state institutions and the *volk*. The upshot is a Civic Truth in which the State is generally seen as bad and Society as good. Human rights are thus defined narrowly as limits on the power of the state (negative liberties) and only reluctantly as involving fundamental socio-economic obligations and individual responsibility.[40] In this characterization, the quality of the public square is a function of society's autonomy from the state. It is but a short step to the generalization that *all* civil societies must be thus defined, irrespective of the diversity of historical and cultural realities. Or as Keane puts it, such idealizations wrongly suppose that 'civil societies are largely unencumbered by self-paralyzing contradictions and dilemmas' – which in turn calls for the need to constantly develop new images.[41]

In that regard, Keane argues that in transitional states that lack civic traditions to enable peaceful democratization, a common recourse is to seek refuge in nationalism or other certitudes of cultural and religious identity; these are as perilous as the certitudes embraced in established democracies, like individualism or the notion of rational argumentation. For they lapse into a reductive 'foundationalist' understanding of civil society, at odds with the pluralism of purpose and commitment that the members of society actually have.[42] In effect, 'the meaning and ethical significance of civil society at any given time and place can be asserted and/or contested as such only within a sociopolitical framework marked by the separation of civil and state institutions, whose power to shape the lives of citizens is subject permanently to mechanisms that enable disputation, accountability and representation.'[43] This, for Keane, is a preference that must override other organizing options, contrary (as seen earlier) to Rorty's willingness to treat civil society as merely one (however desirable) among alternative choices. Otherwise, relativism takes over and undercuts pluralism, in precept and practice.

The modern public sphere, hence, may encompass ethical or ideological frameworks but not the other way round; its boundaries are determined by civic elements alone. That is the only available recipe for serving contemporary diversities of ethnicity, culture, religion, politics and individual purpose – *a fortiori* amid the growing impact of economic and political globalization, which has spawned a transnational, if still inchoate, civic culture. What has yet to be addressed, whether by theorists or activists, is the nature of the relationship between an ethical framework such as Islam's to the kind of public sphere outlined above that is central to modern civil society, while recognizing that varying national and cultural contexts make for varying dynamics on the ground. This takes the discourse beyond the usual question about whether 'Islam' is 'compatible' with democracy or civil society: that line of inquiry simply normatizes Islam – a faith shared by a billion Muslims on every continent – and occludes the complexity of *changing* Muslim intellectual and social life in favour of stock models and images. Rather, the key questions here are about why and how an ethical framework matters in a post-foundationalist (after Keane) understanding of the public sphere. Many of the issues on hand have been grappled with by Muslim thinkers and activists like Abdolkarim Soroush, Mohamed Abdel Jabri, Fazlur Rahman, Rachid al-Ghannouchi, Sadiq Jalal al-Azm, Nurcolish Madjid, Chandra Muzzafar, Mohammed Arkoun, Abdullahi An-Na'im and Bassam Tibi, some of whose works are drawn upon in the remainder of this essay.[44]

IV

There is rich irony in today having to negotiate the nexus between ethics and civic culture past the currents and eddies of 'secularism' and 'religion', and not only in the Cartesian context of Western societies where this dualism has long prevailed amid the ascendancy of the secular. In the *weltanschauung* of Islam, where the sacred and secular (*din* and *duniya*) are merged – and in which some are inclined to subsume the state (*dawla*) – there is a different challenge. Bernard Lewis is among those who conflate the *weltanschauung* with the institutional arrangements of the polity, claiming that church and state are not 'separable' in Islam.[45] This would imply, wrongly, that civic life cannot accommodate a deep regard for the sacred amid such legal/political separation. The real problem has to do with the continuing pervasiveness in Muslim discourses of what Arkoun calls a 'moral totality validated entirely by divine teaching', which is given further public momentum by an attentive media.[46] This tendency in the discourse has less to do with the exercise of moral reasoning that is vital to social ethics, than with nourishing the 'social imaginary'.

What is ironic is that in the classical age of Islam when the leading ethical texts were authored, drawing inspiration both from scripture and the philosophical heritage of the Mediterranean world at large, a moral critique of politics was not seen as a profaning of sacred norms. The pragmatic rationale for the 'Virtuous City' of al-Farabi is the interdependence of human beings in pursuit of self-sufficiency and fulfilment, a *voluntary* quest that ultimately requires the social and spiritual aid of Islamic tenets.[47] Moral traits (*akhlaq*) and habits (*adab*) were individual acquisitions with a social purpose, transcending the public-private divide. *Adab* as a code of dignity and social refinement had ancient roots in the Near and Middle East, into which Islam infused a conscious moral purpose.[48] The upshot was a flowering in the work of, among others, Miskawayh (d. 1030) in *The Cultivation of Morals* (*Tahdhib al-akhlaq*),[49] and its Persian-Shi'i counterpart, *The Nasirean Ethics* (*Akhlaq-i Nasiri*) of Nasir al-Din al-Tusi (d. 1274),[50] which drew conspicuously on Aristotle and neo-Platonist sources.[51] Indeed, writings on ethics caught fire after the translation by Ibn Hunanyn (d. 911) of the *Nicomachean Ethics*, on which al-Farabi was the first scholarly commentator in Arabic.[52] The ethos of the Greek *polis* was subsumed into a new universe where integrity, courage, temperance, charity, justice and reason were virtues that made for individual happiness and the ideal *'umma*. For al-Ghazali (d. 1111) in the *Criterion of Moral Action* (*Mizan al-'amal*), they find expression as more than a set of social and personal rules about right and wrong (*ma'ruf wa munkar*); they become part of the process of moral reasoning.[53]

Yet that aspect of ethics, as furnishing a critique of political and individual conduct, was in contestation with the role of the enacted Shari'a, itself derived from the moral framework of the Qur'an and the Hadith. While al-Ghazali was able to bring his considerable authority to bear in casting a skeptical eye on what he perceived as the ethical deficits of those wielding the enacted Shari'a, the overarching historical trend was of the latter's dominion.[54] The reasons ranged from the need for an authoritative corpus of law over a rapidly expanding Muslim empire, to the political conservatism of Arabia from around the 11th century that led many jurists to affirm the 'closure of the gate of *ijtihad*' (independent legal reasoning).[55] The decline of *ijtihad* was accompanied by a pattern of compartmentalizing law and politics, so that the latter – *siyasa* – became the domain of the caliph or sultan, as an exercise in kingship. The law, in all its potent civic and religious if not intellectual authority, was the domain of the *ulama* or religio-jurists.

Hence, the die was cast for the ruler to seek the collaboration of the *ulama* in an expedient arrangement: the former in pursuit of 'religious' legitimacy, the latter of enhanced political influence.[56] Although this did not preclude ad hoc ethical judgments by communities and individuals about the conduct of civic affairs through to the modern era, the sacralization of the law inevitably curtailed the scope, potency and systematization of such a critique. The potential of ethico-legal principles as *rationes legis* – generalized tenets that lent themselves to application in particular cases – was overshadowed by the spirit of *taqlid*, imitative compliance with a set of specific rules extracted from the manuals of various legal schools.

Since the sacralization of law enhances the legitimacy of political establishments that can invoke it for the exercise of their authority, the tension with those seeking civic accountability is obvious. The hallowed phrase '*siyasa shari'a*' refers formally to the political and administrative facets of the law; but it also signals attempts at sacralizing political power.[57] In post-revolutionary Iran, for example, the constitutional tenet of *velayat-e faqih* (rule of the jurisconsult) confers supra-democratic authority on the un-elected 'supreme religious leader' and renders the clergy and their courts as 'guardians' of the political process, including control over the media.[58] On an even more pervasive level, civic life in Saudi Arabia has been stifled by conservative, intertwining princely and clerical institutions that claim religious legitimacy – and, ironically, face a still more conservative challenge on those very grounds of legitimacy.[59] Elsewhere, the primacy of the Shari'a, as interpreted by traditionalist establishments, operates to trump secular law and effectively circumscribe civic discourse, as witness recent developments in societies as diverse as Egypt and Pakistan, with regard to strictures on blasphemy, apostasy and gender equality.[60]

All of which underscores the need to separate the institutions of state, religion and society, as a shared modern democratic and ethical imperative. That proposition was famously advanced in the 1920s by the Egyptians Ibn al-Jawzi and 'Ali 'Abd al-Raziq, only to run into a wall of orthodox opposition.[61] Yet far from violating Islam's *weltanschauung*, this institutional separation is a means of advancing its civic spirit in practice, and builds on historical realities long manifest in Muslim experience.[62] Secular culture in this respect is an ally rather than an antagonist of religious well-being, with social ethics serving as a bridge between the two in the public sphere. It is in this sense that Abdolkarim Soroush advocates the secularization of ethics en route to modernity,[63] abjuring the 'ethics of the Gods' for 'concrete and accessible rules' that admit of human frailty.[64] Judging by the results of successive Iranian elections since the mid–1990s, in which ordinary citizens have repeatedly and overwhelmingly endorsed the most anti-clerical choices available, it is obvious that Soroush (a key supporter of the 1979 Revolution) speaks to a deep disenchantment with theocratic claims over the public sphere. 'Having freed themselves from the cordon of previously luminous ideologies,' notes one observer, 'many of Iran's intellectuals are now busy articulating serious and sophisticated criticisms of ... authoritarianism, censorship, clientilism, cult of personality, etatism, fanaticism, influence peddling, partisanship, and violence.'[65]

Moreover, sacralizing the law provides no guarantee of the primacy of the rule of law as an institution, identified earlier as a vital element of civil society. Indeed, the argument can be made that sacralization actually undermines the rule of law, since both the content and the implementing institutions *ipso facto* operate outside the framework of democratic/civic accountability in all its contemporary pluralist complexity. It is tantamount to a foundationalist approach of the type explicitly rejected in the preceding segment. The more general problem of the weakness of the rule of law shared by emerging democracies – especially those in post-civil conflict transitions (like Algeria, Azerbaijan, Bosnia, Indonesia, Iraq, Lebanon, Somalia, Sudan and Tajikistan) – only reinforces the 'ethical imperative'. That is, public respect for social ethics acquires the burden not merely of supporting the rule of law, but of actively filling a normative as well as practical gap in the latter's absence or enfeebled condition.

Reliable sociological data on citizen perceptions of civic life in Muslim-majority contexts are relatively scarce, but not entirely lacking. Tair Faradov's seminal survey on Azerbaijan, for example, is instructive about attitudes in transition both from Soviet rule and territorial conflict (with neighbouring Armenia)[66] – conditions not atypical of postcolonial experience in much of the Muslim world. Over 90 per cent of Azerbaijanis opined that religion should not influence politics, but was an important determinant of 'public morality' (84 per cent) and 'culture' (70.6 per cent); this in a country where the majority did not consider themselves observant Muslims.[67] The institutional division of church and state that is written into the country's secular constitution enjoys widespread endorsement, with 'Islam' perceived foremost as an affirmation of personal spiritual and ethical values.

In neighbouring Turkey, according to another recent survey, majorities of 78 to 85 per cent oppose amending the civil code to accommodate Shari'a norms concerning women – yet robust majorities favour social practices like prohibiting the sale of alcohol during Ramadan, allowing exclusively religious marriages, and modest public dressing by women.[68] In both instances, and likely across much of post-Soviet Central Asia and beyond, support for secular culture and religiously-based social ethics is perceived not only as compatible but also as desirable, a trend likely to be accentuated by the events of September 11, 2001, and their aftermath.

More broadly, it bears observing that a symbiotic nexus between law and social ethics is integral to the evolution of modern legal systems, and that a seminal principle of Muslim ethics is respect for the rule of law. Again, if transitional societies often draw upon their ethical heritage to compensate for the weakness of the rule of law, they may also need to do so in terms of solidarity and self-organization – the social capital of civic culture – that are especially necessary when states are weak. Social capital is customarily seen as stemming from engaged citizenship, an elusive expectation in pre-democratic states. Legacies of authoritarian or communist regimes tend to vitiate citizen trust in public organizations and curtail associational life, at least among those who recall the experience of that past.[69] On the other hand, social traditions relating to charitable endowments (*waqfs*), direct and institutional aid through religious tithes (*zakat*) for the disadvantaged, and community-based schools (*madrassas*) have deep roots in Muslim praxis. Regional variants of these include the *mahalla* (neighbourhood organizations) and *gap* (consultative groupings that include interest-free loan associations among women), as well as other indigenous networks whose critical role in post-Soviet Central Asia has been well documented.[70] The potency of these ethical affinities becomes all the more evident in times of crises, when official institutions prove inadequate. This occurred rather conspicuously during the massive Turkish earthquake of August 1999, when mosque-based self-help initiatives were often the principal source of aid for thousands in need of food and shelter in several towns and cities; a militantly secular *devlet baba* (paternal state) was abruptly challenged by the civic efficiencies of 'Islam'. That, at any rate, was the view from official Ankara, which has long viewed religious solidarity groups with the suspicion directed at those demanding equity for Turkey's Kurdish minority.[71]

In comparison with most transitional states in the Muslim world, the Turkish state is relatively strong and Islamist movements in the country do not at this juncture pose a significant threat to the Kemalist Republican *status quo*. What is discomfiting about religiously-inspired ethical critiques from a statist perspective, of course, is their capacity to appeal to sources of legitimacy beyond the democratic framework of the modern polity – especially in transitional contexts when the state's democratic credentials have yet to be fully established. Freedom of the media, judicial independence, clean elections and the probity of public finances, along with secessionist movements and the role of the military, are issues that can profoundly undercut claims to democratic legitimacy. In these circumstances, political accountability may be elicited through appeals to the Shari'a, as has occurred in Afghanistan, Algeria, Iran, Sudan and, to a lesser degree, in Nigeria. The results for individual liberty and civil society have been disastrous, not least because of the sundering of the Shari'a from its ethical roots.

Yet as evinced by the surveys from Azerbaijan and Turkey, even a 'secular' citizenry is cognizant of the civic value of Muslim ethical precepts, including normative expectations of financial probity and consultative policy-making.[72] Hence, to the value of social ethics as a compensatory buffer against the frailty of the rule of law and of formal citizenship in transitional states, can be added its prospective role in fostering public accountability and participatory politics. In states where the primacy of the Shari'a curtails democratic avenues of accountability and participation, an ethical critique may effectively be the *only* available means to challenge the clerical establishment. This has typically been the case at various stages in post-revolutionary Iran, notably with regard to the contest between reformists and conservatives on the status of women. By grounding challenges to male-dominated readings of the Shari'a in wider Muslim notions of social equity and solidarity, Iranian intellectuals and activists have acquired a platform with a competing claim to legitimacy.[73] Thence, such platforms can bridge appeals to more universal norms of human rights and pluralism that would not otherwise get a hearing in such theocratic contexts. Iranian women, for instance, have been actively engaged in United Nations conferences on gender equality – and not merely to influence the latter in favour of conservative interpretations of international human rights law. Rather, progressive global agendas can find expression in otherwise hostile territory through legitimate indigenous actors.

V

If social ethics have an empowering role to play for assorted Muslim publics, they can offer crucial restraints, not only as proto-rule-of-law but also as a compass for appropriate *means* to respond to and foster change. The very notion of a 'civil' society is grounded in opposition to *uncivil* conduct, involving not only disrespect for the rule of law but also the absence of comity and nonviolence. Or as Paul Ricoeur puts it, 'Violence is always the interruption of discourse,' and an articulate violence is already 'trying to be in the right'.[74] Indeed, democratic orders alone offer no assurance of civility, as instanced by the violent 20th-century histories of both eastern and western European states. Taming the impulses of incivility is, in effect, a precondition for civil society – and a task that enjoys '*distinct* ethical status':

Modern societies are able to function because of some reliable expectation of civil treatment among their participants, and this expectation is a normative one. It is what ought to happen: a society is better, more like what it ought to be, if there is a high degree of civility, and such civility is a form of trust and mutual respect or recognition ... Persons *are* entitled to respect as 'moral ends in themselves,' to use Kant's well-known language.[75]

Within a Muslim ethos, this expectation is not merely a pragmatic or functional one but also, in the Kantian sense, moral. Applied in the context of transitions to democracy, amidst the pressures of new global economic and political forces, change rather than continuity is the norm for the majority of Muslim societies. The pace and radical quality of that change may be perceived as a deliberate assault on indigenous values. On occasion, the assault is physical, when politico-economic establishments use the security apparatus of the state to stifle dissent and protest, or to deny the exercise of the right to collective self-determination. The responses by citizens and groups are often also violent, with the rationales drawing on a religious vocabulary.[76] 'Islam' is readily harnessed as a legitimating discourse and ideology that privileges opposition to social, political and economic injustice, while its clear proscriptions against violent reaction are simply discarded. In self-reinforcing cycles of militancy – epitomized by the tragic recent histories of Algeria, Afghanistan and Palestine – the result is to profoundly debilitate the public sphere.

The events of September 11, 2001, and their fallout serve to underscore graphically those patterns of civic subversion. In this political climate, normative frameworks like those of international human rights that outlaw the use of violence to advance claims of justice,[77] can be resisted (if not dismissed) *qua* ideologies emanating from the same Western establishments that collaborate with oppressive governments in the Muslim world. *A fortiori* with regard to transnational criminal law directed at terrorism. Hence, invoking ethical injunctions against violence becomes imperative. I am not, of course, suggesting that such injunctions are a substitute for the rule of law as *cordon sanitaire* for civic culture. Rather, the latter must be an integral part of the revival of dialogical, nonviolent politics as the prevailing ethos.

There is no dearth of Islamic tradition and authority in this regard. 'Whoever slays an innocent soul ... it is as though he slays all of humanity,' is an oft-quoted Qur'anic verse (5:32). Muslims are forbidden from initiating hostilities, and warned when taking up arms in self-defence to 'not transgress limits' (Qur'an, 2: 190). The rationale for jihad was to *limit* the legitimacy of warfare to preserving the loftiest moral values (Qur'an, 4: 75; 22: 40), not to provide an alibi for the discontented.[78] Those moral values could never, for example, include forced conversion: 'There must be no coercion in matters of faith.' (2: 256). Ideologues who claim that Muslims are enjoined to 'slay [enemies] wherever you find them!' (4: 89) tend to overlook not only the defensive context,[79] but also the fact that the same verses insist that if the enemy ceases hostilities, 'God does not allow you to harm them' (4: 90). Repeatedly, Muslims are urged to abjure revenge (5: 45; 2: 192, 193), and to iterate 'Peace' in response to provocation from the ignorant (25:63). The Hadith or Prophetic traditions cherish an even disposition, as in the sentiment: 'The most worthy of you is one who controls himself in anger.'[80]

A key underlying principle, noted in the opening essay, is that an act that violates 'the bounds' amounts, in the final analysis, to an injury against the Self (*ulm al-nafs*).[81] The individual is made inseparable from the Other, the natural and social context in which he is entwined with community and cosmic home alike. This finds concrete expression in the ethos of inclusiveness, compassion and reason conveyed by *hilm* (derived from *al-Halim*, one of God's scriptural names and attributes), that scholars have seen as definitive of Islam:

> In a certain sense the Koran as a whole is dominated by the very spirit of *hilm*. The constant exhortation to kindness (*ihsan*) in human relations, the emphasis laid on justice (*'adl*), the forbidding of wrongful violence (*zulm*), the bidding of abstinence and control of passions, the criticism of groundless pride and arrogance – all are concrete manifestations of this spirit of *hilm*.[82]

In this vein, there ensues a convergence of individual and communal, private and public notions of rectitude. The idea of the *umma* becomes the embodiment of ethical affinity, bridging the sacred and the secular. The ethos at hand is one of principled embrace of civility (as befits a religiously-motivated outlook), which is to be distinguished from a mere tactical adoption of nonviolence (guided by expedient judgment that an adversary can be more effectively dealt with by such means). The importance of that distinction has been underscored by Richard Falk in contexts ranging from post-Revolutionary Iran to eastern Europe and the Philippines: it is ultimately a principled opposition to violence that is required to sustain civic culture.[83] Such a grounding amounts in our time to a global ethic, extending across religio-cultural frontiers. Precisely because that moment so clearly presses itself upon us, argues Falk, it provokes 'widespread fear, foreboding, and a disposition to retreat into the closed and rigid structures of the past, both a traditionalist past and a blinkered secularism that represents a degeneration of the modern impulse toward freedom, reason, and autonomy.'[84]

Certainly that goes some way toward explaining the claims of those who resort to self-serving, decontextualized quotation from scripture and prophetic tradition, in support of political agendas whose legitimacy beggars the sanction of reason, revelation or civilization. That such claims appeal to the socially and politically disenchanted is testimony to their ability to integrate themselves into the framework of cultural identities of Muslim societies. This is endemic to post-Cold War 'discourses of origin' in which multiple affinities are reduced to a single dominant identity, which is felt to encompass a community 'whose unity is constructed upon an imagined nation.'[85] Yet, frameworks of identity cannot be meaningful if they are not also *integrative*, capable of absorbing new ideas and evolving along the way.[86] Which brings us full circle to the need to conceive of ethics as moral reasoning, not normative rule-making and compliance, nor the slave of an 'instrumental reason' that denies the sacred on the basis of an ideological construction of rationality.[87] The burden of such a revival must fall ultimately on the intelligentsia, whose need for spaces of freedom underscores, in turn, the primacy of a civil society safeguarded rather than coerced by the powers of the state.

VI

In sum, the polarity between Muslim and liberal approaches to the public sphere is paralleled by the acute opposition within liberal

discourse on human rights between state and society, which reinforces the marginalization of ethics in the civitas. Liberal praxis has
privileged an amoral rationality in which ethical norms function as
surrogates either for 'appropriate conduct' (denying any judgment
on the basis of the good), or 'rational conduct' (denying any role
for the sacred). In effect, this not only privatizes the moral content
of ethics but also subordinates it to 'self-fulfilment'. The practical
consequence in our time is a veritable cottage industry of ethical talk
that has more to do with 'professionalism' and 'transparency', deemed
to be key public virtues. Contending voices like those of Himmelfarb
and Seligman remain in the wings, and are even seized upon by the
'clash of civilization' warriors on behalf of a patriotism that undercuts
pluralism. However, the limits of rights-talk are beginning to find a
voice amid a growing appreciation of the erosion of civility in the
name of individual autonomy. As Margaret Visser puts it, 'Rights in
some ways resemble polite manners,' for 'they can demand, provided
we are law-abiding, that we should behave as though we recognize the
worth of others; they cannot instill in us regard for anyone.'[88]

For Muslim societies in transition to modern polities, mobiliz-
ing social ethics in the service of civic culture has strategic as well
as intrinsic value. The weakness of the rule of law in these polities
lends obvious pragmatic value to a functional ethical framework,
for state and society alike. Equally, the inchoate institutionalization
of democratic accountability and participatory mechanisms leaves a
serious vacuum in the public sphere, which can be ameliorated by
recognized ethical tenets. That recognition is linked to the legitimacy
that principles of social solidarity, self-help and integrity command
qua Muslim ethics. Those principles enjoy legitimacy even among
citizens who regard themselves as firmly secular or nominally Muslim. Which underscores that there is more than instrumental value in
espousing social ethics that have a religious grounding: there is also
the critical dimension of moral capital, for all its seeming dissonance
in the secular liberal mind. Therein arguably lies the scope to enhance
motivation in taking civility more seriously – amounting to a deeper
regard for the Other that rights alone cannot furnish.

The world's 1.2 billion Muslims are diverse in their cultures and
understandings of Islam. But they share a weltanschauung in which

din and *duniya* (but not the modern *dawla*) are merged, so that both secular and sacred resonate in the public domain. Far from precluding the institutional separation of Mosque and State, this perspective takes no ideological position in that regard: the *umma* can thrive in a plurality of political arrangements. In other words, the occidental liberal conception of civil society is not inimical to Muslim traditions simply because it is wedded to secular space. On the contrary, the primacy of the rule of law, participatory politics, and the integrity of individual membership in a pluralist community are values cherished by both traditions. However, a radical secularity that banishes social ethics from the public sphere is patently inimical to Muslim society, for the moral orientation of individual and *umma* alike are privileged as public as well as private goals. Such a banishment also amounts to squandering potential social capital in the form of citizen-public trust, which enables associational life and civic culture to flourish.

There are, it must be admitted, pitfalls in that ethical privileging in the context of civil society. Pluralism – of culture, thought and life-goals – as well as the capacity of modern states to abuse power, suggest that ethical frameworks should be post-foundational, bounded by principles of democratic and civic commitments, including human rights. Tibi has cogently observed that the underlying challenge in Muslim societies is about relocating civic life from a jealously-guarded 'religious' domain to a cultural-political one that accommodates the warp and woof of modernity.[89] For all the cultural anomie (after Durkheim) that is said to afflict Muslim elites in this Age of Anxiety, the prospects for civic life are unlikely to be enhanced by theologically-led invocations of political or social authority. There is abundant evidence on this score from the contemporary histories of several transitional states, including Afghanistan's post-1995 experience under the Taliban regime, and some of the 'religious' responses to the demise of Saddam Hussein's regime in Iraq.

As well, the rigidities of traditionalism that can reduce ethics to the minutiae of law call for resistance. If Muslim ethics are to occupy a salient position in the civitas, the veins of moral reasoning will need to be tapped beyond turning scripture into political ideology. Indeed, this resonates deeply with Habermas' 'discourse ethics' in his ideal model of the public sphere, wherein capable citizens engage in a communal process of reasoned deliberation on quotidian moral issues. On this basis, the issue of political violence would be confronted in setting the limits of what is acceptable even in response to injustice, when the result is a rupturing of civility and social order in which the *umma* has its being. True, the interdependence of individuals and societies demands an ethos whose frontiers are global and require integrative quests in the civitas; but a welcome ecumenicalism cannot dispense with the need to draw upon and evolve indigenous cultural-religious traditions. For the latter impart incision and substance to the ever-thinning identities and ethical frames of reference of our postmodern age.

Chapter 3

A Humanist Ethos:
The Dance of Secular and Religious

I

John Rawls, the late philosopher of liberalism, famously remarked that religion was a 'conversation stopper': there was nowhere to go when secular logic collided with God.[1] Indeed, the sociologist Emile Durkheim had observed much earlier that 'God, who was first present in all human relations, pulls out progressively, leaving the world to men and their conflicts'[2] – at a time when European modernity was in the throes of consigning both religion and its ethical cognates to the private domain. *Laicité* was enshrined in French law in 1905 to put the Catholic church – and public spaces for moral discourse – in their place.[3] Humanism had come to be defined, against an Occidental heritage once shared with the Islamic world, as an ethos rooted in a secular *civitas* not only institutionally but substantively shorn of the sacred.

While the institutional power of the church was more robust in the historical memory than actual practice of North Americans, the same trend was firmly underway – pursuant to the constitutional 'wall of separation' doctrine. The 1932 case of *United States v. MacIntosh* is illustrative.[4] Douglas MacIntosh was a Canadian citizen who attended the University of Chicago for his advanced degree before making a teaching career with the Divinity School at Yale University in New Haven, Connecticut. He enlisted with the Canadian armed forces during World War 1 as a chaplain, and was in active service. MacIntosh then applied for naturalization in the United States and was asked about his readiness to take up arms in defence of the country. He answered affirmatively, but with the proviso, 'I should want to be free to judge of the necessity.' His religiously shaped conscience was to be the final arbiter in this matter. The matter went before the U.S. Supreme Court, where a majority ruled against MacIntosh on the breathtakingly simple ground that 'the war power, when necessity calls for its exercise, tolerates no qualifications or limitations.'[5]

In vain did the dissenting minority of the Court hold that the constitutional protection of religious liberty and freedom of conscience did not have substance if it could readily be overridden by the state. The embrace of state supremacy over individual conscience remains to this day, from issues of school prayer and public displays of religious symbols, to the pledge of allegiance 'under God'.[6] Even the iconic sportsman Muhammad Ali was sentenced to a five-year prison term for his conscientious objection as a Muslim to serving in the Vietnam War in 1967 (though the US Supreme Court was ultimately to allow his appeal, after the sentence had cost Ali his world heavyweight boxing title in the prime years of his life).[7]

In Canada, political bargaining between Catholic Quebec and Protestant Ontario as a founding reality of confederation meant that religion found plenty of expression in the constitution, a reality taken seriously enough to be preserved beyond the original *British North America Act* into the 1982 *Canadian Charter of Rights and Freedoms*. But while the wall of separation may have been more porous than south of the border – as with state funding of parochial schools – the warp and woof of the public sphere has, if anything, been closer to European secularism. Canadian multicultural policy since 1970 has been premised on ethno-cultural over religious or conscientious pluralism. And in the most authoritative recent survey of public religiosity on every continent, conducted by the Washington-based Pew Charitable Trusts, Canada and Europe ranked at the lower end of the scale. In stark contrast, the United States has twice the Canadian level of expressive religion, more consistent with South American and many Muslim societies.[8] I will revisit this phenomenon, which has far-reaching implications for civic culture.

The prevailing brand of secularization in the West is depicted by Charles Taylor as 'post-Durkheimian', compared with earlier phases in which the individual citizen had a formal affiliation with a given institutional religion ('paleo-Durkheimian'), followed by a phase in which he or she freely chose an affiliation ('neo-Durkheimian').[9] For Taylor, the material difference in our post-Durkheimian age is the replacement of the institutional link between the individual and religion with a strictly personal 'expressivist' preference that glories in the label of 'spirituality'. It matters here because the erosion of that institutional link with religion also means the loss of a connection through religion with the state, since the two are engaged in a dance that defines our secularity in the first place. That dance may have evolved from a tangled tango to contemporary jazz movements, but a dance it has been and still is in most of the world. By contrast, the post-Durkheimian landscape calls for a rap performance – the partner has vanished. After all, the governing ethos here is that of individual human rights. And rights-talk is liberalism's civil religion, displacing the aspirations of moral competence and discourse.

Civil society, whose modern conceivers in the Enlightenment saw it as the edifice of ethics[10] – a status to which it still had serious pretensions in Tocqueville's North America in the 1830s – is effectively being reduced to nothing more than the edifice of the rule of law and the rights of citizenship. This vision enjoys in our time the benefit of export by globalization where possible, and by military means where necessary. I shall return to some of its discontents at home – after venturing into the landscape of the Other that serves as the principal counter to our post-Durkheimian vista. The Other in question, 'Islam', is seen to lack modernity's vital attachments to the rule of law and privatized ethics, in effect, to civic rationality or public reason. This approach to Islam falls squarely within the polarity posited by what Samuel Huntington has cast as a 'clash of civilizations', in which Islam and Muslims effectively inhabit a compartment destined to collide with the Western compartment.[11] The events of September 11 have fuelled that perspective to the point of rendering it the staple of portrayals by politicians, the media and prominent scholars of 'the stakes at hand'. Indeed, the earliest official responses to September 11 insisted categorically that this was all about the integrity of our civilization, which was being subjected to a militant 'crusade' – that's President George Bush's term – which had nothing to do with the content of Western foreign policies.[12]

There is a nuance here that merits attention. Officialdom was asserting *not* that the assaults were simply ethically odious in the extreme and that the proffered rationalizations of those responsible for them could not conceivably justify the acts. That might have been the kind of dignified anger on behalf of the victims – who, incidentally, included some 800 Muslims among the estimated 3,054 killed[13] – in which most of the world could partake without reservation. Rather, we had and still hear the assertion, imbibed widely by mainstream Western media, that the attacks were inspired by nothing more than the irrational rage of the Other, and to question the justice and wisdom of policies that may have fuelled such rage would be to surrender to its irrationality.

In its logic and expediency, this posture brings us to a theme that runs right through the Occidental depiction at large of Islam and the Muslim world. The Rational is tied to secularity as a hallmark of modernity, both as defined by post-Enlightenment experience. Conversely, the rejection of that secular modernity unavoidably yields the irrationality of the Islamic Other. There is no redemptive value to this particular embrace of irrationality, for all the allure of Tradition and its certitudes in a world in extraordinarily rapid flux. No romanticism attaches to the images that spring forth from this benighted universe where women are trampled on as second class citizens, adulterers are stoned, petty thieves have their hands amputated, despotic sultans build palaces and armies from oil wealth that eludes their toiling subjects, and civility is forever at the mercy of anger in the streets.

Indeed, violence is perceived as the single most pervasive trait of this Irrational Other, whether in the confines of one's private sphere or the public square or the domain of external relations. Samuel Huntington invokes this 'propensity toward violent conflict' as vital evidence of Islam's incompatibility with Western civilization[14] – indeed, the very same that gave us intercontinental ballistic missiles, advanced chemical and biological weapons, two world wars and the

Holocaust, the genocide of native populations in grand colonial ventures, Hiroshima and Nagasaki, and urban violence whose casualty rates can rival those in wartime. But I digress.

The point here is that in deploying the term 'propensity', Huntington suggests a disposition, a tendency, a reflex, responses that in the context of modernity can only be devoid of rationality. There is no space here to inquire about what these are responses to, such as grievances about political and economy hegemony, colonial occupation, the brutality of secular rulers whose power is underwritten by Western establishments, and expressions of the crudest racism in words and acts. Nor does the generalization allow for pluralism within the universe of 1.2 billion Muslims, whose cultural heritages are perhaps the most complex and multivocal of any single faith tradition.

The flipside of this is Huntington's plaintive lament about excessive multiculturalism within Europe and America, which he fears is sapping the strength of the West. 'When Americans look for their cultural roots, they find them in Europe,' we are told; the more than one-third of citizens with roots in Africa, Asia, the Middle East and South America need not apply. For its part, Europe must cultivate politico-cultural unity with America or risk becoming 'an inconsequential landmass at the extremity of the Eurasian landmass'.[15] Recall that this analysis came prior to September 11 and the ensuing 'war on terrorism', and the Iraq crisis. It requires little imagination to see how profoundly useful it has since become in the rhetoric and calculus of demonization.

There is, however, a deeper layer of the cultural identity of the Other within which this propensity to violence has been located by scholars like Bernard Lewis, Daniel Pipes and Martin Kramer, before and since September 11. Lewis commands particular attention as an 'authority' on Islam, despite the fact that his corpus of writings shows a proclivity to sweeping generalizations that would seldom pass the test of serious scholarship on Christian or Jewish historical traditions and their political implications. His latest book, *What Went Wrong?*[16] has been almost as popular as Huntington's *Clash of Civilizations* and purports to offer a sophisticated appraisal of historical and political currents in the Muslim world.[17] There have been spin-offs, in the mainstream media to 'educate' the public on what lies behind

September 11, including a lecture by Lewis carried on radio by the Canadian Broadcasting Corporation (CBC), 'The Revolt of Islam',[18] a variation on the title of his article in *The New Yorker*, 'Islam in Revolt'.[19] That famous propensity for violence was again in evidence in Lewis's account but with a twist. This time it stemmed from the doctrine of *jihad*, which was said to be a doctrine justifying aggressive behaviour by Muslims since the time of the Prophet Muhammad. Which is something that one encounters routinely in the popular media, with *jihad* becoming shorthand for just about any kind of violent tendency associated with religion.

The evening before the broadcast of Lewis's lecture, CBC Radio's had aired an instalment of 'Regarding Islam', a series of conversations by the eminent Canadian journalist Don Mowatt in which the London-based Muslim scholar Sheikh Zaki Badawi, and I, explained some of the intricacies of *jihad* – primarily that its association with warfare in defence of religion was explicitly deemed by Muhammad the least important aspect of the concept.[20] For the vast majority of Muslims, *jihad* is foremost an inner struggle with one's *nafs* or baser instincts, the constant battle of conscience and spirit that lies at the heart of any religious quest. Lewis dismissed this perspective in a single sentence as something that Muslims merely claim today in denial of their history. Listeners who were exposed to both broadcasts might well conclude that what Muslims said about their faith was insignificant compared to the opinion of a 'detached' non-Muslim scholar. Further, Lewis treats this *jihad*-as-warfare as a dominant thread in the history of Muslim civilization, which would place it above the heritage of art and culture, theology, ethics and law. For him, Muslims are attached to a millennium-old division of *dar al-harb* (territory of war) and *dar al-Islam* (territory of Islam or peace), with constant warfare between the two. One wonders where in this paradigm he would fit the 25 million or so Muslims who make their permanent home in the *dar al-harb* of the West, or the immense diaspora in Eastern Europe, South America and East Asia. When Lewis acknowledges that Muslim anger has genuine socio-economic causes, he still subsumes all under the 'failure of modernization', and the bottom-line remains a religiously-sanctioned terrorist response to that failure.[21]

In other words, we are back to the clash of civilizations. Even a fine scholar of the humanities like Wilfred McClay, co-editor of the important recent book *Religion Returns to the Public Square*, ends up quoting Lewis in support of the proposition that 'intransigent religions' like Islam have difficulty adapting to a secular modernity because they have 'a rigid, poorly developed understanding of the world, and of its relationship to the ultimate'.[22] McClay apparently is innocent of the allure, among other things about Islam, of Sufi understandings of ultimate realities, and the mystical world of Rumi and Hafiz that continue to attract thousands of his own Christian and Jewish countrymen. Surely it is telling that an entire volume on religion and public policy in the United States, published well after September 11, with plenty of analytical commentary about Islam and the role of religion in foreign policy, fails to include a single contribution by a Muslim scholar. We are offered instead intellectually and historically dubious observations that spurn the benefit of authoritative scholarship by Muslims as well as non-Muslims in favour of facile generalizations and polarities.

II

What, one may inquire, gives an idea like *jihad* – the version that is accompanied by the propensity to violence – such staying power for Muslims ? Why would the likes of Osama bin Laden be able to command the loyalty of so many in his far-flung al-Qaeda organization and its cohorts? The reductive response that we get from Lewis, Huntington and other experts of their ilk can be captured in a word – Shari'a. 'Because war for the faith has been a religious obligation within Islam from the beginning, it is elaborately regulated' – by the Shari'a or religious law, that is, says Lewis. Hence, 'this is a religious war, a war for Islam and against infidels' for bin Laden.[23] Huntington informs us that the 'underlying problem for the West is not Islamic fundamentalism' but rather 'Islam, a different civilization',[24] in which 'a concept of nonviolence is absent from Muslim doctrine and practice.'[25] In other words, the whole matter of violence and *jihad* relate to the body of religious law.

The operative assumption is that Islam enshrines rules and norms of conduct in its Shari'a, which has the binding force of law for all believing Muslims, and that this legal tradition is itself a defining feature of the faith and its civilization. In fact, this perception of Shari'a as law in the modern sense is pervasive in standard Western accounts, and not surprisingly, finds its way into daily media reports about Islam and Muslims. The outstanding characteristic of this law, which is thought to be scriptural, hence its binding force, is thought to be its rigidity. After all, if ancient punishments like the amputation of hands for theft and the stoning of adulterers still hold water, then the underlying code of law must surely be fixed *ad infinitum*. And this brings us full circle to the view that Islam must, therefore, be firmly wedded to tradition and defiant of rationality. This stems not only from blind avowal of tradition but from the very nature of religious law. As Lenn Goodman sees it, Islam gives us an ethos in which God's commands are an end in themselves and this 'opens the door to anti-rationalism' typical of scriptural legal systems.[26]

For these pundits, then, scriptural law defines the identity and conduct of Muslims, and there can be no departure from this code no matter how irrational its consequences. To seal their fate in modernity, that scriptural law is replete with concepts like *jihad*-as-war and other denials of reason, nonviolence and pluralism. After all, there are verses like the following in the Qur'an to support this logic: 'Slay [enemies] wherever you find them!' (4: 89); 'Warfare is ordained for you, though it is hateful unto you' (2:216); and 'Fight against those who, despite having been given revelation before, do not believe in God nor in the Last Day' (9:29). And did not Muhammad proclaim, 'Fight in the name of God and in the path of God'? Pulled out of the wider text and the socio-political context in which these injunctions are embedded, they appear to sanction militancy without end. Certainly that is what Lewis makes of them in his post-September 11 writings:

> Muhammad, it will be recalled, was not only a prophet and a teacher, like the founders of other religions; he was also the head of a polity and of a community, a ruler and a soldier. Hence his struggle involved a state and its armed forces. If the fighters in the war for Islam, the holy war 'in the path of God,' are fighting for God, it follows that their opponents are

fighting against God ... The army is God's army and the enemy is God's enemy. The duty of God's soldiers is to dispatch God's enemies as quickly as possible to the place where God will chastise them – that is to say, the afterlife.[27]

Under the title 'The Roots of Muslim Rage', this essay evinces all the analytical subtlety of a pronouncement by US Secretary of Defense Donald Rumsfeld about what his armed forces will do to the enemies of God's America. It requires a few moments of informed reflection to see that the Qur'an and the Prophet *were not licensing but limiting* the grounds on which, and the manner in which, defensive warfare could be conducted by Muslims. There is an absolute prohibition on 'compulsion in religion' in the Qur'an (2:256), capped by the argument, 'If your Lord had so willed, all those who are on earth would have believed; will you then compel mankind against their will to believe?' (10:99).

When fighting 'in God's cause against those who wage war on you', says the scripture, 'do not transgress limits, for God loves not the transgressors' (2:190). In this vein of defensive war, there are firm injunctions about harming noncombatants as well as women and children, granting safe passage, preserving religious sanctuaries, and the treatment of prisoners (47:4, 8:67, 2:217, 9:6) – remarkably similar in purport, incidentally, to modern humanitarian law as embodied in the Hague and Geneva Conventions. The quote from Muhammad about fighting 'in the path of God' comes from a Hadith – an attested report – in which he sets forth the need for integrity and honour even in adversity, to the point of physical protection for unbelievers if they pay their taxes, and not giving in vain pledges of peace.[28]

War is a last resort, the child not of virtue but necessity: 'The requital of evil is an evil similar to it: hence whoever pardons and makes peace, his reward rests with God. If one is patient in adversity and forgives, this is indeed the best resolution of affairs' (42:40–43). Scholars like Sohail Hashmi, James Turner Johnson and John Kelsay have shown that the ethics of warfare as they evolved in Islam are parallel to the just war doctrines of Christianity.[29] To which might be added the seminal psycho-social readings of scriptural violence in Judaeo-Christian mythos by René Girard in *Le Bouc emissaire* (*The*

Scapegoat) and other studies, which has fed numerous writings in the same vein by Leo Lefebure, Charles Taylor and others.[30]

It is worth noting that the Qur'anic references to conflictual violence pale in comparison with those in Judaeo-Christian scriptures. The Book of Joshua lyrically narrates the killing of 'every living creature' in the name of Yahweh's vision of Israel (10:28–40; 11:14). The Book of Deuteronomy is no less sparing: 'You shall destroy all the peoples ... showing them no pity.' (7: 16), and 'You shall put all its males to the sword. You may, however, take as your booty the women, the children, the livestock, and everything in the town – all its spoil – and enjoy the use of the spoil of your enemy which the Lord your God gives you.' (20:14–15) Christians and Jews, have on occasion taken these verses quite literally despite the provisos of just war doctrines. We have, for instance, this eyewitness testimony of the Provencal Raymund of Aguiles on the aftermath of the First Crusade in Jerusalem, when in the space of three days in mid-July 1099 an estimated 30,000 Jews and Muslims were slaughtered:

> Piles of heads, hands and feet were to be seen ... If I tell the truth it will exceed your powers of belief. So let it suffice to say this much, at least, that in the Temple and the Porch of Solomon, men rode in blood up to their knees and bridle reins. Indeed, it was a just and splendid judgement of God that this place should be filled with the blood of unbelievers since it had suffered so long from their blasphemies.[31]

After there were no infidels left to kill, the Crusaders washed and sang hymns – all this crowned by the recital of liturgy around the tomb of Jesus. The Muslims were soon to have an opportunity to reciprocate and display the 'violence propensity' and *jihad*-as-warfare spirit that Huntington and Lewis credit them with. In her acclaimed book, *Jerusalem: One City, Three Faiths*, Karen Armstrong records otherwise. Saladin led the Muslim reconquest of Jerusalem on October 2, 1187, and no Christians were killed, in keeping with the conqueror's undertaking. Patriarch Heraklius left the city in a chariot groaning under the weight of his treasure, scandalizing the Muslims. But Saladin did not confiscate his wealth: oaths and treaties must be kept, and 'Christians everywhere will remember the kindness we have done them ...'[32]

Meanwhile, Jews were actively welcomed back into the city from which they had been excluded by the Crusaders. They poured in from North Africa and as far away as Andalusia. Yet this return inspired an admixture of gratitude and bigotry. Jerusalem, they insisted, was their city in which Muslims and Christians were making a home. Even Judah Halevi and Maimonides, men of learning who had known the pluralism of Muslim Andalusia, insisted that Jerusalem was sacred to the Jews alone and the proper site of a 'reclaimed' Kingdom with the Temple Mount as its heart.[33] No doubt many would be inclined to dismiss all this as so much water under the bridge. Judaeo-Christian ethics have since metamorphosed into a radically different mould, it might be argued. That is not, however, the interpretation offered in our own time by Yitzhak Shamir, before he became prime minister of Israel:

> Neither Jewish ethics nor Jewish tradition can disqualify terrorism as a means of combat ... We are very far from having any moral qualms as far as our national war goes. We have before us the command of the Torah, whose morality surpasses that of any body of laws in the world: 'Ye shall blot them out to the last man.'[34]

The object here is not to set up a normative or historical contest among the ethical traditions of Christianity, Islam and Judaism. Rather, it is to argue that judgements about the locus of ethics and fidelity to them is complex in all faith traditions, and seizing upon a particular episode or historical phase as emblematic or conclusive in this regard is an exercise in ideological manipulation. It has serious consequences inasmuch as the manipulation can influence not only the drift of general scholarship in the humanities and social sciences (and the task of ethical retrieval against violence within the traditions), but also the opinions of establishment elites that shape public policy and the general public whose support they seek. There are two related elements at work here in the process of depicting the Other. First, as already stressed, there is the construction of a tradition wedded to a rigid legal code, resistant to civility and pluralism as virtues of modernity. Second, there is the assumption which holds that image together, linking Muslim tradition with contemporary behaviour in a determinism – conscious or not – about the impact of tradition on those somehow 'programmed' or 'wired' to passively follow it. Together, these two elements bring me to my central argument, which is that the *content* of the image of the Irrational Other that comes out of the post-Durkheimian West belies the play of ethics and reason in Muslim scripture and historical experience. I will then conclude by considering some of the civic implications of this alternative appreciation of Islam.

III

The opening words of the Qur'anic revelation, dating to the year 610 CE, enjoin the Prophet – and by extension all who encounter the text – to 'Read' in the name of a God 'who teaches humanity by the Pen... that which it knew not' (96:1–5). Thereafter, the text repeatedly exhorts the reader with phrases like 'What! Would you not reason out?' or 'They might perchance reflect!' or 'Perhaps you may exert your mind!' Argument abounds in the verses or *ayat*, as they are called. And the term *ayat* also means 'signs', a double meaning that is no accident. For the act of reading the Qur'an was to be an exercise in discerning the signs of the Divine, unravelling the truths in the *ayat*. The invitation to 'Read', then, was emphatically not the kind of exercise to be pursued without the fullest acuity or proper engagement of the human intellect.

For Muslims, scripture and its attendant civilization from the outset signalled that aesthetics, ethics, human and physical sciences, no less than philosophy and theology, were exercises in discerning 'the signs', *ayat*, in a myriad encounters with the Divine Intellect. The game is played by a text filled, to quote George Hourani, with 'semantic depth, where one meaning leads to another by a fertile fusion of associated ideas.' As such, the scripture is less a doctrinal or juridical text than 'a rich and subtle stimulus to religious imagination.'[35] An example of this – a combination of the dialogical, the ironic and the ethical at the same time – is the *ayat* from Medina when Muhammad and his community, or *umma*, had all the practical burdens of fostering a civic and not just a religious community. The text reads: 'We offered the trust of the heavens, the earth and the mountains to the spirits and the angels, but they refused to undertake it, being afraid. But the human being undertook it – humankind is unfair to itself and foolish' (33:72).

We have a cosmic narrative here from which is derived the concept of human vicegerency or custodianship of nature (*khalifa fi'l-ard*), a trust that makes rigorous demands in perpetuity. For willingly taking this burden on where angels fear to tread, the verses offer a 'tender rebuke' to humans who let pride get the better of wisdom.[36] At the same time, the moral and intellectual capacity to fulfil that trust is also, of course, a divine gift. Frailty, courage and humility are conjoined in this custodianship, which becomes a foundational principle in the development of Muslim ethics. In the graphic 10th-century Arabic fable from the *Rasa'il* (Epistles) of that spiritual and intellectual fraternity known as the Ikhwan al-Safa (Brethren of Purity), a company of animals asks whether human beings are superior to them, and if so then why. They put this question before the king of the spirits (*jinns*), whose verdict is that human beings are indeed superior – yet only for their higher burden as nature's custodians. They are uniquely accountable and must heed the perils at hand:

> Let man not imagine ... that just because he is superior to the animals they are his slaves. Rather it is that we are all slaves of the Almighty and must obey His commands ... Let man not forget that he is accountable to his Maker for the way in which he treats all animals, just as he is accountable for his behaviour towards his fellow human beings. Man bears a heavy responsibility.[37]

The Qur'an's constant challenge to apply intellect and faith to reading, interpreting and acting upon its passages gave birth to an empowering ethos, in which Muslims were encouraged to see themselves not merely as pawns in a cosmic game, but as important players. When the early community finds itself surrounded by tribal practices that violate the dignity of the individual – ranging from female infanticide and the *lex telionis* of blood revenge for killing, to the taking of unlimited wives, hierarchies of caste, and usury – Islam's response could not be one of putting up and letting be. That would be a travesty of the lofty moral aspirations that were ascribed to a person of faith. A social conscience was part and parcel of the larger custodianship of the individual because social justice – the sense of fairplay and balance – was simply the flipside of natural justice, the norms of harmony with the cosmos.

This argument was taken to its logical conclusion by Muslim theologians as early as the eighth century, when the Mu'tazili school began to argue that the tenets of justice, both natural and social, were universal and preceded revelation itself. Indeed, the Mu'tazili philosophers saw no conflict between reason and revelation: they were intertwined in God and His creation, including the mind of man.[38] The intuitive sense of right and wrong (*taqwa* in the Qur'an, which summons it time and again) required rationality as much, if not more, than piety. This is manifest in the literally hundreds of books authored by Muslim philosophers such as al-Kindi (795–866), al-Farabi (878–950) Ibn Sina/Avicenna (980–1037), Hamid al-Din al-Kirmani (d. ca.1020), and the prime neo-Aristotelian, Ibn Rushd/Averroes (1126–98), who gave birth and ascendancy to an intellectual culture that shaped law, ethics, the sciences and the arts. And not only in Islam: Europe was indebted to them for reviving Greek learning and casting it in a new light that fuelled the Renaissance.

A potent illustration of the impact of this age on the notion of a rational ethics in Islam comes from the allegorical tale *Hayy Ibn Yaqzan*, written by Ibn Tufayl (c. 1110–85) in Muslim Spain, in which a child finds himself marooned on an island that has no other human inhabitants. Through his relationships with animals and nature, the boy constructs for himself a set of norms about appropriate behaviour, and proceeds eventually to develop acute philosophical insights about the interplay of the human and divine intellects.[39] But Ibn Tufayl doesn't stop there: the boy's physical isolation mirrors a spiritual loneliness, and engenders a longing for union with the Divine, in keeping with the ideals of the Sufis. When he finally makes contact with the outside world, it turns out that the ethics of the island are congruent in remarkable degree to those of the civilized world, which has a lesson or two to learn from the intuitions of the boy. It comes as no surprise that this allegory is thought to have made quite an impression on Daniel Defoe, the author of *Robinson Crusoe*. Muslim ethics had become a distinct and elaborate discipline by the time Ibn Tufayl wrote his allegory, in the hands of Miskawayh (932–1030), al-Mawardi (974–1058) and al-Ghazali (1058–1111) – all influenced one way or another by neo-Platonist thought as refracted by Arab commentators. Nasir al-Din al-Tusi (1201–74) was to follow with his text in the Shi'i tradition that had imbibed fully both the Sufi and rational philosophical spirit; his *Nasirean Ethics* (*Akhlaq-i Nasiri*) became a standard text for religious institutions.[40] The values of integrity, generosity, solidarity and forbearance (*hilm*) defined the ideal *umma* as both religious and civic association impelled by humane reason.

Among the prime beneficiaries and proponents of this new culture of reason were men of science, from al-Khwarizmi (780–850) who gave us algorithms, al-Battani (858–929) who first wrote of annual solar eclipses, and Ibn Haytham (965–1039) who virtually established optics as a distinctive field of study in the Mediterranean, to Ibn Sina with his *Canon of Medicine* (*Qanun fi'l-tibb*), and Ibn al-Nafis (1213–88) who brought an incisive empiricism to bear on the practice of medicine.[41] The results included the world's very first hospitals, the introduction of paper-making to the Mediterranean which allowed Johann Gutenberg to develop his printing press in the 15th century,[42] Arabic numerals drawing on Indian innovation, and even the earliest systems of commercial credit.[43] Enormous libraries fed this quest, from Andalusia to Cairo and Baghdad, enjoying special status in Islamic culture under the ethical precept of *waqf*, or endowment for public purpose. At a time when the average European collection, usually in a monastery like Cluny in France or Bobbio in Italy, had between 500 and 700 books, the caliph al-Hakam II in 10th-century Cordoba is recorded to have needed a 44-volume catalogue for a library of 400,000 books.[44] That figure is dwarfed by the collections of the Fatimids in Cairo, which on Saladin's conquest in 1171 amounted to 1.6 million books, with over 18,000 on the sciences alone.[45] To put that in perspective, the papal library in Avignon in the 14th century had no more than 2,000 books.

No civilization is without its counter-currents, from within and outside. The free-thinking Mu'tazili school of the eighth and ninth centuries inspired the Ash'aris, a conservative Sunni movement that denounced philosophical speculation in favour of a literalist theology. Its greatest figure, al-Ghazali, not only wrote the *Tahafut al-falasifa* (*The Incoherence of the Philosophers*) but also a highly sophisticated ethical tract, the *Mizan al-'amal* (*Criterion of Moral Action*) and a splendid commentary on the logic of Aristotle.[46] In the midst of political factionalism and the splintering of once-dominant dynasties in the Near East and Central Asia, conservative doctrines that opposed innovation (*bida*) and creative legal reasoning (*ijtihad*) were destined to gain ground. The dominance of al-Ghazali's brand of theology was reinforced by the still-greater traditionalism of Ibn Taymiyya (1263–1328). But not before Ibn Rushd had explicitly countered al-Ghazali with his opus, *The Incoherence of the Incoherence*, which reminds us of the intellectual torch lit by Islam in Spain. For those inclined to dismiss the free-thinkers as occasional spurts in a history of anti-rationalism, or to claim as Lewis does that for Muslims (and Christians) 'tolerance is a new virtue,'[47] is to wilfully misconstrue the historical record. In Muslim-ruled Andalusia from the eighth century to the fifteenth – just as in Fatimid Cairo, Ottoman Istanbul, and Mughal Delhi – the scope of accomplishment from architecture to medicine to philosophy was matched only by the culture of plural-ism that allowed Christians, Jews and Muslims to create a genuine social synthesis. It was this that impelled Hroswitha of Gandersheim, a Saxon writer visiting Cordoba in the 10th century, to call it 'the ornament of the world' – also the title of Maria Rosa Menocal's ac-claimed recent book on the subject.[48]

Another visitor to that kingdom was a Tunisian Muslim whom we today recognize among the originators of the empirical method in his-tory, Ibn Khaldun (1332–1406). His capacity to see the social dialectics of his own faith tradition in the struggles of centres and peripheries within the larger dynamics of civilizational rise and fall, tells us that what makes his *Muqaddima* (*Prolegomena*) a classic of world literature also reflects on the maturity of critical Muslim social thought by the 14th century. Al-Farabi had envisioned in his 10th-century *al-Madina al-fadila* (*The Virtuous City*) a civil society that captured some of the elements in his own milieu, whose ideals were fired by Plato's *Republic* yet fully encased within a religious imagination. Again, al-Kirmani's *Rahat al-'aql* (*The Comfort of Intellect*) had sketched an ideal city that was the product of a spiritual vision. Ibn Khaldun the empiricist was hard on the abstractions of the philosophers; but like the island boy Hayy Ibn Yaqzan, he allowed his astute analysis to sip liberally from the wellsprings of esotericism, because he was also a Sufi.[49] The mix of critical reason and faith is not deserted even in what we might call a 'professional' historical work like the *Muqaddima*.

I draw attention to this, and have dwelt on historical currents, because there are pointers here about Muslim critiques of modernity. Certainly the intimate and painful encounter of Muslims with colonial Europe, and then with America, had the effect of provoking a catch-up attitude where science and technology and political organization are concerned; and a retreat on the part of some into the refuge of religious tradition as the badge of individual identity. But it is well to remember how far back in history Muslim fidelities to rationalism and critiques of it, actually go. Much the same is true of early tides in the histories of pluralism and civility in Muslim cultural experience. To reduce these currents as flowing solely from the encounter with the colonial West is neither accurate nor, as an explanation of deep-seated civilizational intuitions, adequate. For it occludes trajectories into modernity that do not fit into those of the dominant paradigm, such as with respect to secularization, [50] or what the Iranian intellectual Reza Davari deems to be 'Western reason'.[51]

IV

Historical retrieval shows, as the late Fazlur Rahman argued, that in the cross currents of liberal and conservative forces, Muslim ethics have failed to receive due attention as effectively the 'essence' of scripture and much of the civilizational endeavours stemming therefrom.[52] Muhammad is pointedly reminded in the Qur'an that he is one of a line of prophets in the business of delivering a universal message – *hudan li'l-nas* – in which the key moral concept is *taqwa*, the sense of right and wrong.[53] The ethical imperative is distinguished by its pluralism, religious and civic, as in the oft-quoted verses, 'We have made you into nations and tribes that you may know one another' (49:13), and 'If God had pleased He would have made you a single people' (5:48). Specific moral lessons are drawn from universals, and universal inferences from the particular. In recalling the allegory of Abel and Cain, we are warned, 'Whoever kills a human being, it is as if he has killed all of humanity. And whoever saves a life, it is as if he has saved all of humanity' (5:32). This wasn't lost on the Prophet. Christians and Jews were part of the civic *umma* that he constituted in Medina in 622 CE under the world's first formal constitution (see

Appendix A below), accompanied by mechanisms of implementation through consultation (*shura*).

As noted earlier, the supposedly distinct and immutable corpus of Muslim law – often loosely termed Shari'a, which literally means 'the proper path' – is actually a set of ethical guidelines.[54] Neither the language nor the structure of the vast and highly amorphous norms developed from the verses of the Qur'an and Prophetic guidance would remotely serve as 'law' in the sense of enforceable juridical rules. Of the traditional fivefold scale of values in the Shari'a, viz., obligatory, desirable, neutral, reprehensible and forbidden, only the first and last – *wajib* and *haram* are juridical; the rest are ethical. The more specific rules derived therefrom, the *fiqh* or jurisprudence, served the rapidly expanding realm of Islam which needed a rule of law.[55] As in all faith-based systems, the mixture of morality and law gave both legitimacy and a higher motivation to those who lived by it. But as seen earlier in this study, conservative tendencies tamed the role of creative reason that had driven the early development of law. In this context, law and the wider Shari'a often became political instruments for various establishments, of rulers as well as clerics (*ulama*) seeking autonomy from the state. The upshot was that law, such as it was, overshadowed ethics in civic Islam.

That is not to say that the humanistic reason that underpins any ethical system worth the name was dissipated. Outside the formal bounds of *fiqh*, ordinary men and women, as individuals and communities, faced the daily challenge thrown up by the Qur'an to all believers to perform that which is transparently good (*ma'ruf*) and to abjure that which is harmful (*munkar*) (3:104). As an obligation that was both social and personal, this spurred fertile discourses and critiques of the behaviour of establishment elites, political and clerical.[56] While the scope to develop modern rights and obligations in the framework of traditional law was curtailed, the wellspring of ethics remained to contest tradition. Ann Elizabeth Mayer puts it thus in her *Islam and Human Rights*,

> [T]he Islamic heritage comprises rationalist and humanistic currents that is replete with values that complement modern human rights such as concern for human welfare, justice, tolerance, and egalitarianism. These

could provide the basis for constructing a viable synthesis of Islamic principles and international human rights ...[57]

This is precisely the thrust of contemporary civic reform movements across the Muslim world, in campaigns for gender equality in Nigeria and Pakistan, for accountable government rather than clerical dominance in Iran, for tolerance of dissent in Egypt and Syria, for the right to express religious affinities in public spaces in Turkey and the ex-Soviet republics of Central Asia. While orthodox revivalists, whom we call 'fundamentalists' or 'Islamists', invoke the Shari'a or *fiqh* as a criterion that governments must meet, and secular politicians respond by stifling human rights, the middle ground is increasingly occupied by activist intellectuals and their acolytes who appeal to civic ethics. Consider, for example, the popular call by Syria's Muhammad Shahrur for independent reason in reading the Qur'an, to modernize the rules that purport to be derived from it. His 1990 book on the subject became a bestseller for a readership in the secular as well as theocratic regimes of Egypt, Jordan, Saudi Arabia and Syria.[58] And it is obvious that his adamantly pluralist critique lends itself to liberal demands against governments and clerics despite the fact, or perhaps even because, he is not a religiously-trained scholar but a professional engineer.

More directly confrontational has been the dissent of Hashem Aghajari, the reformist Iranian academic who recently risked the death penalty for boldly declaring, 'We are all capable of interpreting the Qur'an without the help of the clergy.'[59] Aghajari has compared the excesses of the 'ruling class' with the worst days of the Catholic papacy. But like Shahrur, he locates his critique firmly within the ethical fold of Islam, in this case Shi'ism. Indeed, the Persian term *rowshanfekran* is often used to characterize these movers and shakers, and it captures accurately the spirit of enlightened thought, religious and secular, that they draw upon. Typically, in a recent critique of the theocratic narrowing of liberal thought in Iran, Abdolkarim Soroush appeals to the ethos of 'an art-loving God' against political tyranny.[60] Which also reminds us how important Iranian cinema has become as a vehicle for a liberating cultural ethos, and the search for a post-Revolutionary identity.[61] Abbas Kiarostami, Majid Majidi, Mohsen and Samira Makhmalbaf, Ja'far Panahi and Bahman Farmanara, for example, are celebrated auteurs the world over with their incisive yet subtle portrayals of repression and longing; while official constraints on viewing their films in Iran are subject to the challenges of a thriving market in pirated videos.

A populist trend is also visible among Turkish activists like Fethullah Güllen and the Nurcu movement founded by the late Bediüzzaman Said Nursi (1873–1960), stressing themes of independent religious thought, tolerance and civic engagement.[62] In a country that is clearly living down the legacy of Ataturk and the dominance of the military as self-appointed guardian of his brand of secularism wanes, it is not fundamentalism that appeals to a society at the crossroads of Europe and Asia but a homegrown, quite liberal Islam. That is what the Nurcu and Güllen have long offered, and what the newly-elected Development and Justice Party (AKP) also claims to represent. Indeed, even the *türban* or headscarf campaign that had earlier been waged in a robustly religious vocabulary and met no success in the courts or the legislature, has come to grips with a human rights discourse as an extension of religious affinity.[63] Again, that affinity is finding expression (and is integral to the AKP's agenda) in a rational ethics of social tolerance, not a demand for 'religious law' to be enacted.

A similar trend developed in Jordan, when a group of civic activists sought to put a stop to the 'honour killing' of women, which the country's legal system effectively condoned by imposing light punishments, if it prosecuted the killers at all. Yet a quarter of all homicides in Jordan have been ascribed to honour killings.[64] The campaign appealed not only to human rights law but also to the ethics of accountability and of 'self-educated' citizenship.[65] The activists made a point of not registering themselves in order to emphasize their political and legal autonomy, yet managed to get royal attention and support, as well as international media and activist interest in a cause that remains a major issue in Jordan.

The appeal to civic ethics is stronger still in war-torn societies, especially where religious extremism was factor in the conflict. In post-civil war Tajikistan, for example, activists like Aziz Niyazi and Daulat Khudanazarov – a former presidential candidate – have been at the forefront of cultural and intellectual renewal to foster a modern civic identity in which the country's diverse Muslim populations can share. Khudanazarov happens also to be a writer, poet and former chief of the union of film directors from the Soviet era. In a country where the rule of law remains frail, I was reminded time and again during my fieldwork there that ethical principles rooted in cultural identity needed to be propagated in schools and in the mass media – a conclusion that one of the leading scholars on the region, Shirin Akiner, endorses as the main hope for civil society.[66] Akiner has also pointed to the remarkable success within Tajikistan of the autonomous Badakhshan region in creating civic institutions that are 'unique' in their sustained commitment to values of self-reliance and volunteerism.[67] Against greater odds, similar activism is underway in Afghanistan, where Sima Samar and Nasrine Gross have been advocating not only for women's rights but a broader liberal culture. Once again, the tenuous hold of the rule of law underscores the dependence on ethical norms to uphold public order as well as commitments to nonviolent change.

V

None of the public intellectuals – *rawshanfikran* – or movements discussed here stand for a merging of church or mosque and state, despite their summoning of faith-based public ethics. Nor are they exclusive in a social, ethnocultural or religious sense. And in response to the question, 'What does it mean to be a Muslim?' it is improbable that any would offer a response that would have been recognizable a mere three to four decades ago. Quite aside from the dynamics of post-colonial and post-Cold War identity, the impact of globalization and the new media is evident virtually everywhere.[68] Of course, Muslim identities three or four decades ago would also have been significantly different from what they were a century ago, at least in urban areas. After all, responses to new colonial and hegemonic Western encounters that were making themselves felt at the dawn of the 20th century were products of different mindsets on the part of the individuals and communities concerned. This may seem entirely axiomatic, yet the larger point is that it wasn't only the social choreography or imaginary that had evolved but 'Islam' itself in terms of what it means to Muslims. The content of Shariʻa and *fiqh* may be stable but the understanding of what these actually mean and how they influence the experience of modernity and tradition, is hardly an *idée fixe*. Rather, it's a function of time, space and circumstance. To speak of 'Islams and modernities' is not only to underscore the experiential and confessional diversity of Muslims today but also to acknowledge the reinvention of tradition itself through history.[69] It means rejecting lock, stock and barrel the underlying claim of that image of the Other as the product of a static Islam in terms either of Muslims being tied to a rigid law, or as permanently removed from their own heritage of humanistic reason.

Ironically, nowhere is a deterministic perspective on Islam less persuasive than in the West itself, where the Muslim diaspora has become a conspicuous feature of the landscape in the past half century. The issues of identity and public religion play themselves out most visibly in contrast and congruence with the most modern host societies – from France and Britain to Scandinavia, the Netherlands, Germany and North America – where they have influenced and been influenced by the law, political economy and sociology.[70] Moreover, globalization and the Internet have allowed the diaspora to interact more than ever with their ancestral communities as part of what Gary Bunt calls the 'digital umma'.[71] The greater access to communications technology in the West[72] means that this diaspora has a vast presence in cyberspace, on satellite television channels and on radio airwaves. In the wake of September 11, 2001, the focus on terrorist networks that use these electronic spaces has obscured the wealth of Muslim discourses that make the digital *umma* a vital universe in today's re-inventions of tradition, as Dale Eickelman and Jon Anderson, among others, have documented at length.[73] Quite apart from the fact that the diaspora itself is as diverse socio-economically and culturally as the Muslim world, it also inhabits secular environments in which expressions of public religion and civil society are not uniform but differ from place to place. The many Islams interface not only with varied modernities but also with Christianities, Judaisms, and so on.

I mentioned earlier the results of the Pew global survey on public religion. What is one to make of the utterly atypical situation of the

United States (home to six million Muslims) as compared with any other Western country, including a leadership that freely articulates its policy objectives in Judaeo-Christian terms in the context of responses to September 11?[74] On the one hand, Jose Casanova argues that the 'process of the Americanization of Islam is already taking place,' in the sense of including symbolic expressions such as scriptural readings, festival meals and the presence of imams at official events in state and federal institutions; there has even been a Muslim chaplain attached to the armed forces since 1993.[75] On the other hand, there is the establishment perspective articulated by William McClay, whom I quoted earlier, and acknowledged by Casanova, that treats Muslims within and outside the United States as an 'out' group in relation to perceived concerns about national security, especially since September 11, 2001.[76] There is the further complexity that, to cite Casanova again, 'Islam has perhaps resisted better than any other religion the modern colonial logic of racialization' in all its 'corrosive' effects on the formation of religious identity among immigrants.[77] American Catholicism gained a profile in direct relation to waves of Irish, Italian and Hispanic migration; Judaism was represented by Central European refugees; Protestantism by North Europeans. Islam fits no such boxes: there have been waves of Afghan, Albanian, Bosnian, Chechen, Indo-Pakistani, Iranian, Iraqi, Lebanese, Palestinian, Somali, Sudanese Muslims, among others, together with large clusters of indigenous African-American and other converts to Islam.

One recalls that multicultural policy in Canada, as in most of Western Europe, is likewise based primarily on ethno-cultural pluralities rather than religious ones. Hence, these modern democracies face a pluralist challenge beyond merely of ensuring that legal and political frameworks meet the appropriate human rights standards of equality on grounds of colour, race and creed. In France with its *laicité* and the Netherlands where officialdom takes a similar position, there is the issue of how secular spaces will accommodate expressions of public religion that are different from those of the mainstream.[78]

The discourse of human rights and civic culture has found fresh respect among Muslims who must depend on the empowerment of citizenship for equality and equity in the diasporas of the West, but clearly also in Jordan, Turkey, Iran, Pakistan, Nigeria and beyond, where ethical discourse meets demands for the rule of law.[79] So much for the rhetoric of orthodox revivalists who dismiss human rights as an 'alien' idea, until of course they require its protection against secular despots. Or the claims of Western relativists and orientalists who ascribe to an ahistoric, monolithic Islam a rejection of anything modern, from human rights to civil society. Yet the secular liberal rights ethos has been subjected to a range of sobering criticism from within – above all, for polarizing the individual and society in the quest for liberties that must ultimately be shared if they are to have meaning, and which can't mean everything in and of themselves. The discontents include voices across the ideological spectrum: Stephen Carter, John Gray, Gertrude Himmelfarb, Robert Putnam, Michael Sandel, Charles Taylor, Margaret Visser, Michael Walzer, to name a few. From a rights perspective, Ronald Dworkin has assailed a long-standing principle of individualism that lies at the heart of liberal theory: the assumption that harm to others is the primary criterion of tolerance and liberty. This claim is only tenable, he notes, 'if we limit harm to physical injury to person or property,' ignoring that a 'community has an ethical environment, and that environment makes a difference to the lives its members can lead.'[80]

Perhaps it is the impulses of globalization and technology, with their levelling of difference that stems from the local and personal, which have driven a countering tendency in recent decades to emphasize minute variations among groups and nations, the results of which have included genocidal conflict.[81] But for Canada's Chief Justice, Beverley McLachlin, the underlying element is 'the inescapable human need to construct one's identity within a social context'.[82] So, armed with our distinguishing attributes, we bind ourselves to others who share them. Yet if groups are vital for social purposes, they also exclude when they include – which is why we require human rights to create 'protected space for difference within society; a space within which communities of cultural belonging can form and flourish under the broad canopy of civil society.' Still, McLachlin observes, what protects difference goes beyond law. 'Inclusion and equality cannot be achieved by mere rights,' but rather by drawing on values that prize accommodation, and 'attitudes of tolerance, respect and generosity.' Her assertion of a 'universalized ethic of respect and accommodation' is meaningful because it finds expression not just in formal legal and political institutions and norms, but in a myriad acts by citizens in contexts that are local and global. The public spaces in which this sort of accommodation occurs cannot be defined solely by categories like 'secular' and 'religious', which fail to capture the intertwining purposes and motivations of active citizenship that generates the social capital of civil society. Nor in the present climate of heightened political tensions has the rule of law alone protected either individual citizens or entire societies from arbitrary exercises of power by ostensibly accountable governments – as Muslims know first-hand in the diaspora and in the Islamic world. A landscape that recognizes the intertwining of secular and religious, the ethical and the legal, resonates with the ideals of Muslim activists and intellectuals cited here. But it is only a realizable goal if a pluralist ethic of inclusion and rational civic dialogue is consciously pursued, and not left to the vagaries of national life (as discussed in the final essay below).

For all intents and purposes, it has become quite untenable to speak of 'Islam and the West', much less 'Islam versus the West'. The plurality of Islams and modernities demands that we speak of 'Islam in the West' compared with, say, 'Islam in Central Asia' or 'Islam in South Africa'. Equally, we ought to recognize that it is Muslims we actually refer to when we speak of 'Islam' in context – individuals and communities, not ciphers or automatons – whose identities and aspirations are as pluralist as the world itself. This may not please the clash-of-civilization warriors or those who persist in clinging to fixed images of the Other. But it would be ethically – as opposed to politically – correct.

Chapter 4

Pluralist Governance

I

For reasons that stir poetic justice with plain analytical reason, it seems appropriate to begin this essay with Iraq. Amidst disorder in the aftermath of conquest, and widespread demands for the establishment of the rule of law and justice, there are cries also for vengeance from various quarters. The land and its assets are expected to be treated in accordance with international custom as conqueror's booty, a proper reward for those who prevailed in stages over assorted territorial tribes and alliances, until the fall of the Arabian heartland to Islam. Yes, I refer to the year 637 CE, when it was anticipated that the Caliph 'Umar would conform to the authority of the ancient custom that was continued in the lifetime of Muhammad, who had passed away five years earlier. If 'Umar had indeed followed that precedent, his fidelity to the letter of the law – as would later be embodied in the emergent Shari'a – would have been unquestioned. Yet he chose to depart from it, on the grounds that prior practice within patches of Arabian tribal territory was not applicable in the conquest of entire nations like Iraq. Did not the Qur'an emphasize reconciliation and fairplay among, different parties, in the name of a larger brotherhood (Sura 59:7–10)? The Shari'a as 'code' was not fixed: its spirit must reign over the letter, and there would be no land-grab in Iraq.[1]

One could interpret this as legal pluralism, the willingness to embrace different readings of the law in accord with context and circumstance. More cogently, it serves to demonstrate the overriding importance of the ethical Shariʻa, the wellspring of equity and humanism from which springs the law, offering a compass when the law alone seems inadequate. Either way, it throws into perspective a vital aspect of Muslim civilizations that tends to be obscured in contemporary discourse about the public sphere in which ethno-cultural, gender and other minorities seek equality and pluralist expression. In Islam, as in modernity at large, it is the rule of law that is deemed the primary anchor for civil society, the mark of a mature democratic polity, entirely overshadowing the role that ethics once played and ought to do today in governance (*al-hukm*).

Governance here is about the capacity of public institutions to effectively represent all sectors of society – across lines of economic, gender and minority status – with ultimate accountability to the people themselves. The key measures of effectiveness here include transparency, equity and the rule of law, responsiveness and strategic vision.[2] These indices find rich expression in Muslim traditions, as already noted in this study, and in the array of terms derived from the Arabic root *hukm*, denoting judgement among people in the context of mediating and upholding an equitable social order. One recalls that the provisions of the Charter of Medina, promulgated by Muhammad in 622 CE, sought to establish pluralist governance as an imperative for the founding civic *umma* (Appendix A). Further, the critique of humane governance as spelled out in the sermons and writings of Muhammad's companion and son-in-law, Imam ʻAli ibn Abi Talib, extends beyond the formal political sphere to religious institutions: the underlying ethos of accountability and inclusiveness applies across the public sphere, broadly construed.[3]

Notions of procedural and substantive justice, wisdom and accountable rule all link directly with the term *hukm*. It is instructive that the transitional executive and legislative authority in postwar, occupied Iraq was styled the Majlis al-Hukm or Council of Governance[4] – and that a prominent critique of its status invoked precisely the precepts of justice, wisdom, integrity and pluralism, as well as the Medina Charter, as key measures of institutional credibility.[5]

Likewise, in the context of transitional Afghanistan, a sensitive appreciation of 'Islamic governance' has been called for in constructing a representative constitutional framework that accords with indigenous measures of integrity and accountability.[6] Far from positing the unqualified embrace of all things traditional, these critiques recognize that ethico-civic values embedded in faith traditions are ignored at the peril of quests for bona fide democratic modernity.

This essay is centred on three cardinal propositions. First, that pluralist governance is a quintessential prize for the public sphere, and requires a rule of law that is favoured by an ethos of separation of Religion and State (a proposition which is alien neither to Muslim theology nor civilizational experience). Second, that the rule of law in all its potency still requires an engagement with ethics to deliver a meaningful pluralism, evidence of which is no less clear for diaspora Muslim minorities who have lately discovered the limits of human rights protection in so-called advanced democracies, as it is for those who live in war-torn societies where the shelter of the law is fragile. Finally, that the interplay of social ethics and the law can make the encounter of Islam and the West profoundly enriching in facing the shared critical challenge of civic pluralism, again not only in the Muslim world but also in the Western diaspora. The prospect for cultural synthesis on this score is, of course, antithetical to the 'clash of civilizations' industry in which a host of academics and political militants alike have made boisterous careers in the past decade.

Since the end of the Cold War, the world has rediscovered civil society in the public sphere as the cultural and institutional precondition for democratic life. Simply having elections under a paper constitution that proclaims the separation of powers is not a panacea that delivers democracy, even with the imprimatur of observers and advisers from Brussels, New York or Washington. Legitimacy is more complex than that, at least in the eyes of the citizens on whose behalf it is asserted. For modern civic culture to thrive, individuals and communities require the public spaces that are created when the State and its organs are separated from Society itself, whose autonomy renders public life civic and not merely political. That was the key insight of 18th and 19th-century thinkers like Adam Ferguson, John Locke and Hegel, in the wake of the separation of Church and State. They understood that in a society deprived of autonomy, the State would simply swallow its citizens, as occurs most conspicuously under totalitarianism.[7] The rule of law was needed to keep the State accountable, make civic life secure, and protect the individual from both the State and Society so that he or she could be an effective civic actor.

What is 'civil' about all this is the 'attitude of attachment to the whole of society ... of concern for the good of the entire society,' says Edward Shils. It is the 'conduct of a person whose individual self-consciousness has been partly superseded by his collective self-consciousness.'[8] Civility, then, is a trade-off: the citizen commits to the well-being of others who are not only connected by kinship, tribe or religion but also as fellow citizens, who in turn make the same commitment to the integrity of the whole process that safeguards the individual. Not surprisingly, this idea of a community of mutual support was seen as more than a pragmatic or legal arrangement: it was also about social solidarity, which made it an ethical construct.[9] As such, it resonates for Muslims, since an ethos of solidarity, of civility as engagement in the collective good, and of accountability of the governors to a moral code, is precisely what the Muslim *umma* has been about since Muhammad gave it civic expression soon after his arrival in Medina in 622 CE.

II

If the point of civic culture is to trump differences of ethnicity, culture, religion, political ideology and what have you, in favour of common citizenship, then pluralism is an inherent objective – whether in the secular Western or Islamic perspective. Or at least a certain degree of pluralism, on a scale where acknowledging diversity is the starting point, recognition and respect is the next stage, and effective engagement is the culmination. There is a tendency to conflate these evolving phases into catch-all terms like 'tolerance' and 'recognition', which obviously capture important facets of the process. They fail, however, to do justice to pluralism as a willed and difficult quest that aims not at a reductive commonality of assimilative values (which would deny diversity) nor mere compatibility (which amounts to passive tolerance).[10] Rather, the inclusive result yields an 'achieved definition of community', an identity stemming from the interaction of its constituent parts.[11] The appreciation of pluralism as a dynamic continuum beyond passive recognition is not only critical per se, but also links it to social capital, the networks of engagement that give substance to civil society.

A civic culture that fails to make progress on that scale can only have a partial claim to civility, solidarity and accountability. It is intriguing that even Alexis de Tocqueville, writing so penetratingly on American civic culture in the 1830s, failed to put the question of social inclusion at the heart of his extensive critique: women, African-Americans and Native Americans conspicuously fell by the wayside.[12] At the end of that century the U.S. Supreme Court saw fit to rule that the segregationist doctrine of 'separate but equal' was consistent with the Constitution;[13] it required nearly six decades for the Court to acknowledge the ethico-legal fraud in the argument.[14] The same was generally true of the practice, if not the rhetoric, of civil liberties elsewhere in the West. It is a trite observation that formal equality has not meant economic and social – much less attitudinal – equality in practical terms. Yet minorities, women and other disadvantaged groups found in the rule of law a profoundly significant recourse to engineering equity as a measurable work in progress. The effectiveness of this mechanism has had everything to do with the separation of powers that allows the weak, whether in numbers or status, to resist the tyranny (ideological, legal, economic) of the strong.

This is hardly a novel idea for the Muslim mind. The Prophetic quest was nothing if not a struggle against an assortment of tyrannies, from those of tribal and economic status to the endless corruptions of *nafs* (the baser human instincts). Pluralism is hard-wired into the Qur'an, which time and again proclaims that an inclusive *umma* is the only legitimate community of the good, that the very idea of 'Islam' encompasses the Judaeo-Christian heritage, and that there can be no compulsion in religion. This was reflected in the life of Muhammad, who once saw fit to respectfully rise to his feet in the midst of a conversation while a Jewish funeral was in progress, and upon being asked why by his companions, retorted, 'Is he not a human soul?'[15] The pluralist recognition of the Other in Islam goes beyond passive acknowledgement. The Qur'anic verse, 'If God had pleased He would have made you a single people' (5:48) is echoed in the first part of another much-quoted verse, 'We made you into nations and tribes,' (49:13) but the second part of that verse, 'that you may know one another,' takes the fact of diversity to another level. It requires mutual engagement to know the Other, and this is made to be the purpose of the diversity. The implication is that knowing the Other is part and parcel of fulfilling the divine will as spelled out in the Qur'an, and therefore of being Muslim and indeed human in the fullest sense.

This resonates with the wider setting in which the individual Self is located in Muslim cultures. The Self is very much a social being, with a web of family, community and societal attachments. It is not the utterly private, cordoned-off and atomized Self that we associate with the modern West.[16] As such, the Muslim Self with its social, pluralist ties is the flipside of a community that must honour each individual as part of an inclusive social web – which brings us back to the notion of civility as an exercise in civic solidarity. Where practice falls short of principle in ensuring that community and society are indeed inclusive, the secular fallback, as we have seen, is on the rule of law. And the integrity of the rule of law in turn depends on its being independent from the control of the political or the social sphere. This is often thought to be problematic for Muslims, since the secular and the sacred – *duniya* and *din* – are merged in a holistic worldview that is central to Islam. Can Muslims uphold this principle and yet sustain a commitment to the rule of law as a secular institution severed from religion? How can non-Muslims, or for that matter Muslims, who do not share the prevailing readings of Muslim religious codes, find the necessary space for their civic freedom?

The logic here is slippery. Separating Religion and State in terms of institutional arrangements is a matter of practical politics. It is not something that scripture and the Shari'a is concerned about. On the contrary, it is precisely the sort of matter that Muslims have historically treated as part of the mundane universe that is to be tolerated rather than prioritized.[17] Far more salient both normatively and experientially has been the *umma*, whether as the community of believers or the inclusive civic body in Muslim society. The merging of *din* and *duniya* is about how the community perceives itself, how its members look upon each other and the world outside. In other words, it is an ethical concept, not a constitutional or legal tenet.

Not only is there no tangible impediment in Islam to the institutional separation of powers, but further, Muslim political ethics pointedly cherish respect for the law to safeguard public space and civic virtue. Anthropologists have often remarked on the level of public security in marketplaces and other public precincts in the poorest Muslim contexts – explicable only by the effectiveness of ethical rather than legal restraints. In the turmoil of Iraq after the American-led invasion, amid the breakdown of urban infrastructure and public order, the most conspicuous exception to the norm has been the disciplined placidity of men and women massively assembled for sermons in the precincts of mosques, often to be rebuked for misbehaviour in the absence of law enforcement.

There are, of course, some egregious examples to the contrary: a culture of 'war-lordism', often with narco-trafficking undertones, has prevailed in post-conflict Muslim zones in Kosovo, Afghanistan and Tajikistan. But the fact that the response in 'religious quarters' to these breakdowns tends to be focused on this ethical deficit reminds us that they are exceptions to the norm. The Taliban, for example, sought to justify their rise to power precisely in the name of public order against the depredations of war-lordism during and after the Soviet invasion – until they, too, became warlords and faced the opprobrium of much of the Muslim world for their civic and religious intolerance.

An obvious question that arises, then, is if the rule of law is so central to safeguarding civic culture, and this is recognized by secular and Muslim paradigms alike, and if inclusive participation is built into the very foundations of civil society, then why has pluralism been so elusive in practice? I am not referring only to emerging or post-conflict situations where ethno-cultural relations have broken down. Even supposedly mature, multicultural democracies like Canada and the United States repeatedly grapple with failures of pluralism, large and small. Of late, the issue of 'racial profiling' of citizens from predominantly Muslim countries as part of the 'war on terrorism' has raised fundamental questions about the integrity of the rule of law, which requires equal treatment of individuals in public policy. It is rather telling that when the city of Toronto was subjected to a travel advisory by the World Health Organization (WHO) on 23 April 2003, because of the level of Severe Acute Respiratory Syndrome (SARS) contagion there, official Canada reacted angrily at what was perceived to be the equivalent of quarantining an entire city in response to a handful of infections whose provenance could be clearly traced; the ban was lifted with effect from 30 April.[18] Yet the same logic is routinely applied in profiling Muslims and subjecting all the citizens of particular Muslim countries to constraints under North American anti-terrorism policies. By this rationale, all Canadians would be subject to rigorous health checks and restrictions whenever they travel across borders, provincial and national!

What does it say about the health of civic pluralism that the general public and the media are so muted about the treatment of minorities despite having all the facts – which is more than could be said about the SARS situation? How much have we really progressed from the time when North Americans of Japanese ancestry were interned en masse during World War II? One is mindful as well of policing conduct in our own day toward those of African ancestry in urban centres like Toronto and New York. Or consider the refusal of the Ecole de Technologie Superieure in Montreal to provide prayer spaces for Muslim students, contrary to the practice at other academic institutions in the city.[19] The Quebec Human Rights Commission is at this time considering the Muslim students' complaint of discrimination, and the response of the ETS that accommodating their request would violate the separation of Church and State, despite the requirement of 'reasonable accommodation' in Canadian human rights law – a position that it says it will defend all the way to the Supreme Court of Canada.

A province whose 'French fact' has involved grappling longer and deeper than any other with the perceived and actual challenges of cultural pluralism might be expected to be especially sensitive to its own minorities. On the contrary, when the Quebec Superior Court recently found that a Montreal school's refusal to accommodate the wearing of a Sikh ritual *kirpan* (ceremonial dagger) by a 12-year old student, Gurbaj Singh, was discriminatory, the provincial government served notice that it would appeal the ruling even though neighboring

Ontario had changed its policies to accommodate such elementary needs a decade ago.[20]

Then again, consider what happened when Ziyad Yasin, a 22-year old biomedical engineering student at Harvard University, hailing from Chicago, was invited to deliver a commencement speech in June 2002. Yasin took as his theme faith and citizenship, with the subtitle of 'Jihad' that would serve to illuminate his understanding and that of his colleagues of how the Muslim idea of 'striving' fed his intellectual and spiritual commitments. His reward ranged from death threats and harassment to aggressive lobbying of the university's administrators to have him scratched from the list of speakers. Hilary Levy, who led the campaign against Yasin, claimed that she could only visualize 'planes flying into a building' when she heard the word 'jihad'[21] – which, one would have thought, was exactly the reason why she and others needed to hear him.

Harvard's president, Larry Summers, who approved the content of the speech, gave into pressure to have the word 'jihad' removed altogether from the title. Clearly, it was not only freedom of expression that was at stake here but also the freedom of inquiry and thought – with particular regard to minorities. Indeed, as I argued at the time in a *Globe and Mail* article, what this case has in common with the Quebec *kirpan* episode is that both involved an abuse of the separation of Religion and State, whose purpose is to safeguard secular space for pluralism.[22] Instead, the separation became an ideological weapon against pluralism.

There is an intriguing comparison here with the recent ordeal of the Iranian academic, Hashem Aghajari, who encouraged his students and ordinary Iranians to interpret the Qur'an and Shi'i theology for themselves rather than passively follow the interpretations of the clerical establishment.[23] For this he incurred a death sentence for bringing religion into disrepute – a finding that Aghajari refused to appeal since he felt that he was upholding the finest intellectual traditions of Islam. With the robust support of the reformist movement, two-thirds of parliament, and President Mohammad Khatami himself, Aghajari was reprieved. In this instance, the particular *merging* of Religion and State into a theocracy was felt to be threatened by the challenge to the authority of the clerics, whom the Constitution gives political authority under the *velayat-e faqih* (rule of the jurisconsult) doctrine. But in all three cases, civic pluralism was betrayed under the guise of safeguarding the rules that govern the relationship between Religion and State. Whether in the name of secular or sacred space, civility and public reason were shattered. The rule of law did not come to the rescue of Hashem Aghajari or Ziyad Yasin, and it may or may not in the end protect Gurbaj Singh's free exercise of religion in Quebec. Nor has it prevented the adoption of policies and practices of racial profiling of Muslim migrants and residents in overt and subtle forms in the United States and Canada.

III

These cases bring us to the proposition that the rule of law needs the support of public ethics for civil society to deliver pluralism. What is commonly referred to as 'the sense of justice', the intuitive reflex of right and wrong – which the Qur'an repeatedly invokes as *taqwa* (piety) and the associated term *birr* (goodness) – lies behind the rule of law. It is the reason why Islam is said to merge the secular and the religious, the point of which is to have a constant ethical critique of the secular. It relates directly to the Prophet's instinctive reply when asked why he stood up for a Jewish funeral: the deceased was human, and that connected him to every Muslim. The next step for Muslims in the Qur'an is, as mentioned earlier, to know the 'other' – the essence of the pluralist quest. It happens to resonate with the idea of civic engagement as the source of what policy-makers and scholars call 'social capital', which is what civil society is said to generate. Social capital as the outcome of a dynamic web of individual and institutional relations is the currency of public trust that empowers democratic life, culturally, economically and politically. It assumes the existence of the rule of law, but depends on the ethical sense to drive the everyday acts of civility that make citizenship worthwhile.

Where trust is high, diversity among citizens is valued rather than feared, and adds to the sum of social capital. Typically, in apartheid South Africa, for example, socio-cultural groups had zero mutual trust because the law and its ethos were designed to deny common citizenship. If you as an individual felt that this was unethical, your response could only be private: there was no space for the public expression of your sentiment. The same is true for dissidents in a totalitarian system: since conformity is enforced by law and politics, their ethical critique is private. Muslim identity in Soviet Central Asian contexts like Tajikistan and Uzbekistan was not a meaningful thing: ethnic identity was recognized because it suited the state as an instrument of control, but religious identity was private. In other words, diversity was recognized as a strictly formal reality, with no pluralist implications.

No wonder the former Yugoslavia collapsed into ethno-cultural war after independence from the Soviet Union. The question was constantly posed: how could a nation that Josip Broz Tito had kept together without overt ethnic conflict so suddenly turn to genocidal war in Bosnia, Kosovo and Croatia? To ask this is to confuse managing diversity, if totalitarian control can be called that, with pluralism. There was no civil society in any real sense in the Soviet Union because all public space was political, not civic. And you cannot have *bona fide* citizen engagement without civic space. The danger, though, is to assume that where you have civic space safeguarded by the rule of law, diversity will necessarily resolve itself into civic pluralism. After all, it would appear rational to believe that where you create the conditions for inclusive participation to occur, by giving all citizens and their cultural identities proper constitutional recognition and the equal protection of the law, then you have a pluralist democracy. But if this were the case, then Britain would not still be struggling with Catholic-Protestant strife in Northern Ireland, or Canada with the perennial problem of effective federalism that accommodates Quebec, or Spain with the issue of Basque separatism.

Some have characterized the problem as being one of 'illiberal democracy', that is, of excessive reliance on the mechanics of participation through electoral means, with insufficient attention to securing the rule of law from ideological mischief. This is the thrust of Fareed Zakaria's penetrating critique in *The Future of Freedom*, which draws attention to the gap between political liberty and democratic practice not only in transitional societies in Eastern Europe, Asia and Latin America, but also the United States.[24] Yet the assumption here appears to be that liberty and social equity are ultimately a matter of efficacious law and governance, in spite of all the historical evidence of their limits in being able to deliver on an inclusive and civil society. The failures on this score in Northern Ireland, Quebec and Spain can scarcely be explained by profound deficits in the rule of law and liberal culture.

There is a useful clue as to why civic pluralism is such an elusive prize when one considers the analysis of Samuel Huntington with regard to multiculturalism in the United States, in the wider context of his *The Clash of Civilizations*. Huntington laments that what North Americans have in common with Europe – that is, the values of Christianity, pluralism, individualism and the rule of law – is under severe assault and that social capital is in decline. He singles out for criticism 'the encouragement of diversity', which is cast as undermining the social fabric of the United States.[25] 'When Americans look for their cultural roots, they find them in Europe,' he insists[26] – at a time when African, Asian and Hispanic-Americans constitute more than a third of the overall population.

Indeed, this discomfort with pluralism is what underlies the worldview that engenders the 'clash of civilizations' thesis. The entire project of strengthening social capital, the essence of civil society, rests on the premise of a unitary culture and civilization that streamlines diversity into a narrow understanding even of Occidental or Western civilization. Moreover, Huntington and his fellow travellers expect other cultures and civilizations to do likewise within their frontiers. Never mind that no civilization is so territorially self-contained and unitary in its history, values and outlook, least of all the relatively late-coming Western one that includes a melange of Chinese, Indian, Arab, African and Byzantine heritages. The point here is that one has a simultaneous affirmation of civility and the rule of law, and a denial of civic pluralism because it is thought to undermine social capital. And this was prior to the events of September 11, 2001, with all the paranoia and arbitrary public policy measures toward minorities that have been taken in the name of ' homeland security'.

There is a counterpart to this view in parts of the Muslim world, and it is far more complex than a label like 'fundamentalism' can capture. Whether in Afghanistan, Iran, Iraq or Saudi Arabia, to take a few instances, there are many who assert that civic space should be unitary in the sense of being defined by a dominant cultural ethos that resists the onslaught of Western secularity and values, but to a certain degree respects the existence of other cultural minorities within that space. The Iranian Constitution of 1979, for example, accords recognition and parliamentary representation to non-Muslim minority citizens as groups (Christians, Jews, Zoroastrians) as well as individuals, in addition to the general principle of equality before the law.[27] But this tolerance, which does not extend to groups that are not designated, is not quite the same as civic pluralism. Rather like Huntington's preferred paradigm of America, it envisions muted minority citizenship in the name of ideological values that are determined paternalistically by establishment elites.[28]

When these tolerated minorities make demands relating to language use and public expressions of religion that might be seen as contesting mainstream ways, they risk clampdowns of varying force. Often, national security is perceived or cast as being at stake, requiring minorities to reach an accommodation with the political establishment – which, in turn, can spur a backlash when the establishment itself changes. Consider the difficult status of the Kurds in Turkey, for example, the hitherto favourable one of Christians in Iraq, the dramatically changing fortunes of Lebanon's Shiʻa, Sunni and Maronite communities, or the 'managed pluralism' of Indonesia and Malaysia.[29] In an age of globalization and contested social values, diversity tends to find what is regarded as its most progressive management in the discourse of human rights. This is rendered all the more necessary by the resistance that traditional 'honour' codes throw up to pluralist values, in defence of communal identity and patriarchy.[30]

Clearly, there are limits to what the cold letter of the law, even when it enshrines fundamental human rights, can achieve beyond formal equality for individuals and communities. This was recently articulated by none other than the Chief Justice of Canada, Beverley McLachlin, in delivering the annual La Fontaine-Baldwin Lecture which she entitled 'The Civilization of Difference':

> True equality requires an honest appraisal of actual similarities and differences – an understanding of the context in which human devaluation occurs. To make equal worth a reality we need more than what Michael

Ignatieff calls 'rights talk'. We need to look beyond the words to the reality, or context of the individual and group, to understand the other in his or her full humanity. This requires ... a willingness to bridge the gap between groups with empathy. Only when we look at the member of a different group in this way are we able to give effect to the promise of equal worth and dignity ... Inclusion and equality cannot be achieved by mere rights. But when the rights reflect a nation's values and are accepted as a means of brokering our differences and finding accommodation, they take on profound importance. And when we add to the mix attitudes of tolerance, respect and generosity ... the prospects become bright for the inclusive society of which we dream.[31]

What the Chief Justice calls 'attitudes of tolerance, respect and generosity' are, in fact, close to the Muslim understanding of social ethics – the mix of *adab* and *akhlaq*, custom and propriety – that are grounded in the fundamentals of Islamic civilization.[32] They not only are the handmaiden of the rule of law, but the underlying ethos which gave birth to those entitlements that privilege human dignity and which we now cherish as human rights. The intersection of ethical and legal obligation *qua* civic deontology harkens to the origins of modernity, in the influential writings of Hugo Grotius (1583), Pufendorf (1632–94) and Christian Wolff (1679–1754), the articulation of liberty by John Stuart Mill (1806–73) and – against the currents of utilitarianism that followed – in W.D. Ross's *The Right and the Good* (1930). In Muslim and other faith-based contexts, deontological ethics have always trumped the consequentialist logic of utilitarianism. It is a fidelity that has come to find new enthusiasm even in secular approaches to civic ethics, as this study has frequently noted. If civic culture without pluralism is a failure of civility, the rule of law without an incisive framework of ethics can amount to a failure of pluralism – a price too high to pay in an age when our 'civilization of difference', as McLachlin sees it, requires inclusion and engagement beyond tolerance. But how are we to get there from here?

IV

We certainly cannot get there by *imposing* civil society and pluralism with brute force. There is an inherent contradiction in the notion that uncivil means will produce civil outcomes. In Iraq after the second United States-led Gulf War, it comes as no surprise that there is so much civic resistance, on the part of the Shi'i and Sunni Muslims alike, to having an occupying power seek to determine the nature of the future polity and the manner in which civic life is structured. Certainly Iraq needs all the assistance that it can get, as do post-civil war societies like Afghanistan, Bosnia, Kosovo and Tajikistan. But in the aftermath of an invasion that violated the Charter of the United Nations, rode roughshod over the principles of the 1949 Geneva Conventions on the conduct of hostilities and the treatment of civilians, and whose motives have been impugned as grossly unethical, it is not particularly persuasive for the occupying powers to be preaching about the rule of law and civility in public life.

One tends to forget that building modern civil society with a modicum of respect for pluralist principles required the better part of the 18th, 19th and 20th centuries for the countries of the North Atlantic region. It is a labour that Muslim societies, especially those ravaged by postcolonial strife, will have to engage in as a long-term project rather than an overnight objective. Shortly after the end of the Cold War, Vaclav Havel, the Czech intellectual-activist and then president, saw the quest this way:

> There is only one way to strive for decency, reason, responsibility, sincerity, civility, and tolerance, and that is decently, reasonably, responsibly, sincerely, civilly, and tolerantly ... A moral and intellectual state cannot be established through a constitution, or through law, or through directives, but only through complex, long-term, and never-ending work involving education and self-education ... It is a way of going about things, and it demands the courage to breathe moral and spiritual motivation into everything, to seek the human dimension in all things. Science, technology, expertise, and so-called professionalism are not enough. Something more is necessary. For the sake of simplicity, it might be called spirit. Or feeling. Or conscience ... A state based on ideas should be no more and no less than a guarantee of freedom and security for people who know that the state and its institutions can stand behind them only if they themselves take responsibility for the state – that is, if they see it as their own project ... [33]

More recently, in the wake of the events of September 11, 2001, the imperatives of pluralism as a quotidian challenge of civic cultivation rather than a vague expectation of coexistence amid ethno-cultural and ideological difference have come to the fore. A prominent Muslim leader, the Aga Khan, drew attention to this at a European gathering where the expectation among elites may have been that the problem at hand is essentially one for Muslim societies, not 'advanced' democracies.[34] On the contrary, he observed, 'global cultural ignorance' is a keen enemy of genuinely participatory politics 'where an informed public plays such a central role,' in the wider context of nurturing strong pluralist cultures.[35]

Although the institutional separation of Religion and State is generally understood as necessary to foster public spaces that accommodate all minorities, this does not extend to building a wall of separation between ethics and the rule of law. Muslim intellectual-activists like Mohsen Kadivar and Abdolkarim Soroush in Iran, Nurcolish Madjid and Abdulrahman Wahid in Indonesia, Sadiq Al-Azm and Mohammed Shahrur in Syria, Saad Eddin Ibrahim and Nawal Sadawi in Egypt, Daulat Khudanazarov in Tajikistan, Chandra Muzaffar and Farish Noor in Malaysia, Sima Samar in Afghanistan and Ayesha Imam in Nigeria – to name but a few – strive for secular spaces while invoking ethical as well as human rights critiques of the failings of their governing elites and institutions. Social ethics not only lends legitimacy to their critiques in the eyes of fellow citizens, it also avoids depending on the formal commitments of the law alone, which cannot deliver pluralist culture. Further, when the institutions of the rule of law are still in the formative stage, in terms of ensuring independent judiciaries, and full legal accountability of elites to the constitution, the ethical framework is even more vital as the fallback for maintaining public order and dignity. It is a mistake for the outside world to leap to the conclusion that civic activists who invoke Muslim ethics are therefore theocrats in the Western sense. The Persian term *rawshanfikran* is often applied to public intellectuals in the Muslim world, and it invokes perfectly the sense of rational thought coupled with the search for enlightened answers that is their quest. Typically, at a protest against severe constraints on press freedom in Iran, Kadivar uses the symbolism of the pen in Islamic tradition to cast the law as violating a higher ethic,[36] while Morocco's Fatima Mernissi draws heavily on *adab* on behalf of democratic liberalism.[37] One recalls that Western discourse of this order itself had much to do with building the roots of civil society.

Again, as McLachlin and Havel have observed, the liberal paradigm of pluralist civil society itself has been found not to rest on human rights and constitutional traditions alone. A recent book edited by Hugh Heclo and William McClay, *Religion Returns to the Public Square*, throws up a powerful corrective to the earlier lament of Richard Neuhaus, Stephen Carter and others that religion had been left out of the American public sphere.[38] But it is not public religion that is the issue for a pluralist civic culture; it is the ethical upshot of religion. Minorities often prefer a nakedly secular public sphere because it is felt more likely to guarantee neutral civic space for all. The social anthropologist and stalwart observer of Islam and civil society, Ernest Gellner, believed that Islam was so 'secularization-resistant' that it would forestall the development of civil society at all in Muslim-majority contexts.[39] But here Gellner confused secularism as ideology – embraced by the West – with secularization, the plain sociology of modernity that encroaches on all societies, including the Muslim world.[40] The distancing of Religion and State, with the establishment of an effective rule of law, happens in the realm of secularization. It does not require Muslims to abandon the view that secularism, as a doctrine of seeing the world in contestation with the sacred, is to sacrifice the ethical heritage that imparts strength to civic culture, and with the right admixture of human rights, to pluralism.

In this regard, the Muslim diaspora in the West is uniquely placed to draw upon the strengths of both the Western experience of the culture of rights, including its limitations for minority citizens, and the Islamic with its normative commitment to *adab*, *akhlaq* – and the Qur'anic *taqwa* and *birr* – as the soul of public and private religion. In one sense, this has happened conspicuously with former exiles being highly influential, if not actually taking the helm, in post-conflict Muslim societies like Afghanistan and Iraq, not to mention Iran before and after the 1979 revolution. And there are the itinerant public intellectuals whose influence knows no borders, like Mohammed Arkoun, Tariq Ramadan, Hamza Yusuf, Abdullahi An-Na'im, Amina

Wadud, Ali Mazrui, Khaled Abou El Fadl and Abdulaziz Sachedina. However, the actual daily civic experience of settled Muslim communities in Britain, Canada, France, Germany, the Netherlands and the U.S. can impact powerfully in direct terms and by example the shaping of a pluralist ethos at home and abroad. The notion that the 'centre' lies in the Middle East and everywhere else is the periphery is not only outdated but reversed in the age of globalization, where information technology and the media are among the key determinants of the balance of civic power.

Diaspora communities find themselves countering two potential marginalizations. In their adopted countries, hostility toward inclusiveness of Muslim identities and socio-cultural contributions – especially post-September 11 – is not merely a question of recognition in the political sense, but of effective, pluralist citizenship. At the same time, diaspora communities cannot help but seek to influence the unfolding discourse on democratization in their ancestral countries and elsewhere in the Muslim world, as part of what has come to be called the 'digital umma.'[41] In effect, this is about pluralism in the most comprehensive sense, covering not just ethnicity and culture but also geography and ideas.

On both fronts, the domestic and the global, diaspora Muslims have important allies within the West itself, and they are the growing numbers of those from within the Judaeo-Christian tradition as well as others that share the concern over the distancing of ethical principles from the public square in the name of secularism as ideology. From Charles Taylor, Jose Casanova and Hans Küng, to Amitai Etzioni, Richard Falk, Michael Sandel and Amartya Sen, to name but a handful, there has been a withering critique of the old liberalism on behalf of a turn – some would say a return – to civic ethics. Far from being an elitist discourse, it echoes a general public discontent with the alienations of secularist modernity. I don't mean 'secular' in the sense of institutional separation of Religion and State, but 'secularist' in the sense of throwing the sacred out of the public sphere.

Muslims have resisted this banishment of the sacred as a precondition for modernity – without necessarily resisting modernity, as those of a fundamentalist inclination have often done. And those of us who occupy that middle ground between an insistently secularist modernity, on the one hand, and an equally insistent traditionalism on the other, have a common cause to make and strive for – a civic jihad to launch, one might say – in the pluralist quest of civil society. This countering of the shallow 'clash of civilizations' thesis is not really a novelty. It was experienced in the past in a variety of cultural settings, from Cordoba and Fatimid Egypt to Mughal India and the Ottoman Empire, where Christian, Jewish, Hindu and other communities made common cause with Muslims. The thrill of that quest is captured in the Turkish writer Orhan Pamuk's extraordinary novel, *My Name is Red*, set in the late-16th century Ottoman courts, where a community of artists is engaged in a lethal dance of creativity and death as it faces the challenge of the Italian Renaissance. I want to conclude with an extract from a fateful argument between a master painter, Enishte, and one of the younger, highly talented but fearful painters, who accuses the old master of borrowing too readily from the Venetians, especially by using the technique of perspective, which removes the painting from a high, divine view and 'lowers it to the level of a street dog,' and corrupting the purity of Muslim artistic traditions.

Enishte has this to say in response:

> [W]henever a masterpiece is made, whenever a splendid picture makes my eyes water out of joy and causes a chill to run down my spine, I can be certain of the following. Two styles heretofore never brought together have come together to create something new and wondrous. We owe Bihzad and the splendor of Persian painting to the meeting of an Arabic illustrating sensibility and Mongol-Chinese painting ... Today, if men cannot adequately praise the book-arts workshops of Akber Khan in Hindustan, it's because he urged his miniaturists to adopt the styles of the Frankish masters. To God belongs the East and the West. May He protect us from the will of the pure and the unadulterated.[42]

That final sentiment from the Qur'an is affirmed in the creative ethics of pluralist encounters that, in our time as in earlier ones, must counter the temptation to sacred purity and its civic costs. René Girard has explored various dimensions of this tendency where those who are perceived and cast as impure outsiders become scapegoats for ritualistic and other forms of sacred violence.[43] The counter-narrative of solicitude for the victim, Girard observes, is also part of Christian theology – as, of course, is its long history of militant contestation against both Islam and Judaism.

Islam, too, puts the victim/outsider in various normative shelters: as *dhimmi* or protected minority, for instance, or as proper beneficiary in the *adab* and *akhlaq* codes of compassion and generosity. The overriding orientation is toward theo-civic virtue as the only legitimate criterion of inclusion/exclusion in *hukm*, broadly construed.[44] On occasion, there is a permissive departure from that threshold: in the Hadith quoted earlier on the Prophet's solemnity upon witnessing a Jewish funeral, the sole criterion for inclusion is being human, rather than a member of the *ahl al-kitab*, the 'people of the Book'. This orientation attenuates barriers against inclusion by privileging a disposition of tolerance toward social difference, and indeed (as noted earlier) of rational knowing of the Other. Normatively, as Fazlur Rahman has observed, Muhammad is asked to say, 'I believe in whatever book God may have revealed,' (Qur'an, 42:15), for 'God's guidance is not restricted to any nation.'[45] Inasmuch as 'book' here signifies 'the totality of divine revelations',[46] an ethos of dignified accommodation concerning the individual's most central beliefs becomes integral to Islam.

Yet scripture and civilizational norms cannot deliver pluralism; only a lived ethics of engagement by ordinary citizens can. The record of Muslim societal conduct in this regard has often fallen far short of its normative paradigm. This is scarcely unique to Islam, nor is it less true of the claims of contemporary secular paradigms. Deep civic alienation, and its cognates of racial and religious persecution, coexists with sophisticated public policy frameworks of multiculturalism and anti-hate legislation. There appears to be a persistent failure to grasp that this has much to do with normative and policy approaches that are premised on a deficient understanding of what pluralism amounts to. Typically, the prominent American academic, Nancy Fraser, author of numerous works on social justice, argues that the underlying problem with prevailing multicultural strategies is that they favour recognition of group identities over citizenship-based equity of participation.[47] This is a widely heard refrain, of course, in liberal discourse. Fraser, however, contends that the better alternative is to embrace a justice-based model for purposes of both recognition

and redistribution of resources to empower minorities *and* to reject
the ethical foundations of these claims to equity. Her logic is that
aiming for 'parity of participation' is a matter of breaking down 'in-
stitutionalized patterns of cultural value' that 'misrecognize' (exclude,
disparage or otherwise fail to honour) minorities, which in turn is a
problem of justice not ethics.[48] We are back, then, with a full-blown
reliance on the rule of law to deliver pluralism.

The dichotomizing here of ethics and human rights as absolutes in
distributive justice and recognition is precisely the kind of thinking
that I have contested in this study. For it overlooks the role of social
values that must accompany normative principles and rights-talk in
equitable governance and the ensuing legalization of ethical values.
Ironically, it is the very pluralism of contemporary secular societies
that feeds the liberal impulse to abandon value-consensus in favour of
a 'residual' legal consensus, often at the constitutional level, no matter
(perhaps because of) the deep disagreements on the substance of the
compromise involved. But the *modus vivendi* comes at a price: the law
confers its imprimatur, as a prominent ethicist observes, 'in establish-
ing the values and symbolism of a secular society,' effectively making
courts and judges the clerics of today.[49] This implicates a plethora
of issues that engage the foundations of individual and collective
identity, from race and religion to innovative biomedical options,
where the law becomes a moral arena that it effectively converts into
a rule-making one. In a further twist, judges are expected to set aside
their 'personal convictions' as a condition for adjudicating fairly in
pluralist contexts. It is one thing to contend that this is the default
mode for a secular culture committed to civility, quite another to
justify it as the proper recourse to ethical governance.

Nor is this the only questionable turn in Fraser's reasoning, which
also assumes that there is no more to pluralism than formal respect
and recognition, of 'parity' before the law. It was in the recognition
of the *limits* of legal parity in protecting and empowering minority
communities – as opposed to individual citizens – that multicultural
policies were instituted in diverse societies in the first place. Civic
spaces for cultural freedom in all its plenitude, from expressions of
linguistic to those of religious rights, require a governing ethos large
enough to accommodate affinities beyond individual citizenship.

In a secular culture of intense individualism,[50] it is unlikely that claims even to basic tolerance and equity on behalf of groups and communities that do not enjoy ideological favour will find support. The aftermath of the events of September 11, 2001, have shown this vividly enough when it comes to Muslim communities in many parts of Europe and North America. France and Germany have moved, for example, to constrain individual religious expression such as the wearing of Muslim headscarves in public schools – reminding us, as with American public policy in the 'war on terrorism', that grave abridgements of human rights may come in 'liberal' guises.[51]

It is surely too late in our shared histories of misrecognition to set the threshold at tolerance and individual equality, which for minorities like African-Americans, Jews and Muslims as citizens of 'mature' democracies has long meant passive *intolerance*. Public apologies for the more egregious acts of misrecognition have been scarce in the civitas, in part no doubt because of the legal implications; again, retrieval is called for that gives moral substance to pluralism.[52] Repeating the errors of these histories on the emerging civic landscapes of the Muslim world, from Bosnia and Kosovo to Indonesia, Afghanistan, Iraq and West Africa, would be inexcusable. It would also be rather unambitious in light of Islam's own historical capacity for inter-faith civic engagement.[53] Cast in terms of Pamuk's portrayal of the dialectics of civilizational exchange, it is as if the Persian, Turkish and Mughal-Indian miniaturists imbibed the Renaissance innovation of perspective, and then confined it to a dim corner of each painting as their legacy. What a triumph that would be for the will of the unadulterated!

Appendix A

The Charter of Medina (622 CE)

In the name of God, the Merciful, the Compassionate.

This is a writing of Muhammad the prophet between the believers and Muslims of Quraysh and Yathrib [Medina] and those who follow them and are attached to them and who crusade (*jahadu*) along with them.

1. They are a single community (*ummah*) distinct from (other) people.
2. The Emigrants of Quraysh, according to their former condition, pay jointly the blood-money between them, and they (as a group) ransom their captive(s), (doing so) with uprightness and justice between the believers.
3. Banu 'Awf, according to their former condition, pay jointly the previous blood-wits [penalties for bloodshed], and each sub-clan (*ta'ifah*) ransoms its captive(s), (doing so) with uprightness and justice between the believers.
4. Banu'l-Harith, according to their former condition, pay jointly … (as 3).
5. Banu Sa'idah… (as 3).
6. Banu Jusham… (as 3).
7. Banu'n-Najjar… (as 3).

8. Banu 'Amr b. 'Awf... (as 3).
9. Banu'n-Nabit... (as 3).
10. Banu'l-Aws ... (as 3).
11. The believers do not forsake a debtor among them, but give him (help), according to what is fair, for ransom or blood-wit.
12. A believer does not take as confederate (*halif*) the client (*mawla*) of a believer without his (the latter's) consent.
13. The God-fearing believers are against whoever of them acts wrongfully or seeks (? plans)* an act that is unjust or treacherous or hostile or corrupt among the believers; their hands are all against him, even if he is the son of one of them.
14. A believer does not kill a believer because of an unbeliever, and does not help an unbeliever against a believer.
15. The security (*dhimmah*) of God is one; the granting of 'neighbourly protection' (*yujir*) by the least of them (the believers) is binding on them; the believers are patrons (or clients – *mawali*) of one another to the exclusion of (other) people.
16. Whoever of the Jews follows us has the (same) help and support (*nasr, iswah*)(as the believers), so long as they are not wronged (by him) and he does not help (others) against them.
17. The peace (*silm*) of the believers is one; no believer makes peace apart from another believer, where there is fighting in the way of God, except in so far as equality and justice between them (is maintained).
18. In every expedition made with us the parties take turns with one another.
19. The believers exact vengeance for one another where a man gives his blood in the way of God. The God-fearing believers are under the best and most correct guidance.
20. No idolater (*mushrik*) gives 'neighbourly protection' (*yujir*) for goods or person to Quraysh, nor intervenes in his (a Qurayshi's) favour against a believer.
21. When anyone wrongfully kills a believer, the evidence being clear, then he is liable to be killed in retaliation for him, unless the representative of the murdered man is satisfied (with a payment). The believers are against him (the murderer) entirely; nothing is permissible to them except to oppose him.

22. It is not permissible for a believer who has agreed to what is in this document (*sahifah*) and believed in God and the last day to help a wrong-doer or give him lodging. If anyone helps him or gives him lodging, then upon this man is the curse of God and His wrath on the day of resurrection, and from him nothing will be accepted to make up for it or take its place.

23. Wherever there is anything about which you differ, it is to be referred to God and to Muhammad (peace be upon him).

24. The Jews bear expenses along with the believers so long as they continue at war.

25. The Jews of Banu Awf are a community (*ummah*) along with the believers. To the Jews their religion (*din*) and to the Muslims their religion. (This applies) both to their clients and to themselves, with the exception of anyone who has done wrong or acted treacherously; he brings evil only on himself and on his household.

26. For the Jews of Banu'n-Najjar the like of what is for the Jews of Banu 'Awf.

27. For the Jews of Banu'l-Harith the like...

28. For the Jews of Banu Sa'idah the like...

29. For the Jews of Banu Jusham the like...

30. For the Jews of Banu'l-Aws the like...

31. For the Jews of Banu Tha'labah the like of what is for the Jews of Banu 'Awf, with the exception of anyone who has done wrong or acted treacherously; he brings evil only on himself and his household.

32. Jafnah, a subdivision (*batn*) of Tha'labah, are like them.

33. For Banu'sh-Shutaybah the like of what is for the Jews of Banu 'Awf; honourable dealing (comes) before treachery.

34. The clients of Tha'labah are like them.

35. The *bitanah* [close friends] of (particular) Jews are as themselves.

36. No one of them (? those belonging to the *ummah*) may go out (to war) without the permission of Muhammad (peace be upon him), but he is not restrained from taking vengeance for wounds. Whoever acts rashly (*fataka*), it (involves) only himself and his household, except where a man has been wronged. God is the

truest (fulfiller) of this (document).

37. It is for the Jews to bear their expenses and for the Muslims to bear their expenses. Between them (that is, to one another) there is help (*nasr*) against whoever wars against the people of this document. Between them is sincere friendship (*nash wa-nasihah*) and honourable dealing, not treachery. A man is not guilty of treachery through (the act of) his confederate. There is help for (or, help is to be given to) the person wronged.

38. The Jews bear expenses along with the believers so long as they continue at war.

39. The valley of Yathrib is sacred for the people of this document.

40. The 'protected neighbour' (*jar*) is as the man himself so long as he does no harm and does not act treacherously.

41. No woman is given 'neighbourly protection' (*tujar*) without the consent of her people.

42. Whenever among the people of this document there occurs any incident (disturbance) or quarrel from which disaster for it (the people) is to be feared, it is to be referred to God and to Muhammad, the Messenger of God (God bless and preserve him). God is the most scrupulous and truest (fulfiller) of what is in this document.

43. No 'neighbourly protection' is given (*la tujar*) to Quraysh and those who help them.

44. Between them (? the people of this document) is help against whoever suddenly attacks Yathrib.

45. Whenever they are summoned to conclude and accept a treaty, they conclude and accept it; when they in turn summon to the like of that, it is for them upon the believers, except whoever wars about religion; for (? = incumbent on) each man is his share from their side which is towards them.

46. The Jews of al-Aws, both their clients and themselves, are in the same position as belongs to the people of this document while they are thoroughly honourable in their dealings with the people of this document. Honourable dealing (comes) before treachery.

47. A person acquiring (? guilt) acquires it only against himself. God is the most upright and truest (fulfiller) of what is in this docu-

ment. This writing does not intervene to protect a wrong-doer or traitor. He who goes out is safe, and he who sits still is safe in Medina, except whoever does wrong and acts treacherously. God is 'protecting neighbour' (*jar*) of him who acts honourably and fears God, and Muhammad is the Messenger of God (God bless and preserve him).

* The question marks in brackets indicate the ambiguous meaning of certain words in the Arabic document.

Appendix B

The Aga Khan Development Network: An Ethical Framework

The AKDN Mandate

The Aga Khan Development Network (AKDN) is a contemporary endeavour of the Ismaili Imamat to realise the social conscience of Islam through institutional action. It brings together, under one coherent aegis, institutions and programmes whose combined mandate is to help relieve society of ignorance, disease and deprivation without regard to the faiths or national origins of people whom they serve. In societies where Muslims have a significant presence, its mandate extends to efforts to revitalise and broaden the understanding of cultural heritage in the full richness of its diversity, as the quality of life in its fullest sense extends beyond physical well-being. The primary areas of concern are the poorest regions of Asia and Africa. The institutions of the Network derive their impetus from the ethics of Islam which bridge the two realms of the faith, *din* and *duniya*, the spiritual and the material. The central emphasis of Islam's ethical ideal is enablement of each person to live up to his exalted status as vicegerent of God on earth, in whom God has breathed His own spirit and to whom He has made whatever is in the heavens and the earth, an object of trust and quest.

Din and *Dunya*

A person's ultimate worth depends on how he or she responds to these Divine favours. *Din* is the spiritual relationship of willing submission of a reasoning creature to his Lord who creates, sustains and guides. For the truly discerning, the earthly life, *duniya*, is a gift to cherish inasmuch as it is a bridge to, and preparation for, the life to come. Otherwise it is an enticement, distracting man from service of God which is the true purpose of life. Service of God is not only worship, but also service to humanity, and abiding by the duty of trust towards the rest of creation. Righteousness, says the Qur'an, is not only fulfilling one's religious obligations. Without social responsibility, religiosity is a show of conceit. Islam is, therefore, both *din* and *duniya*, spirit and matter, distinct but linked, neither to be forsaken.

The Guidance of the Imam

The challenge of choice is moral and individual, but meaningful in a social context. For while personal morality is a paramount demand of the faith, Islam envisions a social order which is sustained by the expectation of each individual's morally just conduct towards others. The function of ethics is to foster self-realisation through giving of one's self, for the common good, in response to God's benevolent majesty.

By grounding societal values in the principle of human moral responsibility to the Divine, Islam lifts the sense of public and social order to a transcendent level. The lasting legacy of the Prophet Muhammad is the strong suffusion of the mundane, of daily life, with the sense of the spiritual. This prophetic example remains a source of emulation for Muslims everywhere, in every age. Within Shi'i Islam, it is the mandate of each hereditary Imam from the Prophet's progeny, as the legatee of the Prophet's authority, to seek to realise that paradigm through an institutional and social order which befits the circumstances of time and place. In a world of flux, the Imam gives leadership in the maintenance of balance between the spiritual and the material in the harmonious context of the ethics of the faith, of which he is the guardian.

Ethical Foundations of AKDN Institutions

Notionally, the AKDN seeks the ideal of social action, of communitarian strategy, to realise the social vision of Islam. Although the outcome of its action is pragmatic, the motivation for it is spiritual, a universal ethic whose purpose is to elicit the noble that inheres in each man and woman. The abiding traits which define this ethic inform the principles and philosophies of AKDN institutions: their collective focus on respect for human dignity and relief to humanity; the reach of their mandates beyond boundaries of creed, colour, race and nationality; their combined endeavour towards empowering individuals, male and female, to become self-reliant and able to help those weaker than themselves; their policy of nurturing and harnessing a culture of philanthropy and voluntary sharing of time and talent; the transparency of their governance based on the values of trust, probity, equity and accountability; and their overall aim generally to seek to engender, or contribute to other efforts which seek to engender, a fraternal ethos of enlightenment, peace, 'large-hearted toleration,' mutual aid and understanding.

What are the abiding traits of Islam's ethical ideal which inform the AKDN mandate?

Ethic of Inclusiveness

Islam's is an inclusive vision of society. The divine spark that bestows individuality also bonds individuals in a common humanity. Humankind, says the Qur'an, has been created from a single soul, as male and female, communities and nations, so that people may know one another. It invites people of all faiths to a common platform, to vie for goodness. The Prophet sought to harness individual and group differences and talents to serve common needs of different religious groups, among whom he encouraged a spirit of harmony and toleration as constituents of a larger community of his time.

Ethic of Education and Research

The Prophet and Hazrat 'Ali

The key to the nature of society that Islam espouses is an enlightened mind, symbolised in the Qur'an's metaphor of creation, including one's self, as an object of rational quest. The very first revelation to the Prophet is a command to read. Those who believe and have knowledge are the exalted ones. Such cannot be equated with those who are ignorant. 'My Lord! Increase me in knowledge,' is a cherished prayer it urges upon the believers, men and women alike. Learning ennobles, whatever its source, even if that be distant China, and is obligatory upon every Muslim man and woman, the Prophet is reported to have said. 'One's greatest ornament is erudition,' and 'the most self-sustaining wealth is the intellect' which 'gives one mastery over one's destiny,' are among the sayings attributed to Hazrat 'Ali, the first Shi'a Imam. 'Knowledge is a shield against the blows of time,' wrote Nasir-i Khusraw, an eleventh-century Iranian poet-philosopher. But the person of knowledge and wisdom carries the greater obligation of sharing it. The Prophet likens the knowledge which is kept from others to a girdle of fire round one's neck. 'One dies not,' said Hazrat 'Ali, 'who gives life to learning.'

Early Muslim Scholars

The teachings of Islam were a powerful impulse for a spiritually liberated people. It spurred them on to new waves of adventure in the realms of the spirit and the intellect, among whose symbols were the universities of al-Azhar and Dar al-'Ilm in Fatimid Ismaili Cairo and their illustrious counterparts in Baghdad, Cordova, Bukhara, Samarqand and other Muslim centres. Reflecting the spirit of the culture which honoured the pursuit of knowledge, al-Kindi, a ninth-century philosopher and student of Greek philosophy, saw no shame in acknowledging and assimilating the truth, whatever its source. Truth, he wrote, never abases. It only elevates its seeker. As a result, sciences flourished in their different domains: mathematics, astronomy, botany, medicine, optics, pharmacology, zoology and geography. In his *History of Science*, George Sarton traces, from 750 onwards, an unbroken stretch of six centuries of Muslim pre-eminence in the world of science.

The Spirit of Inquiry

Scientific research was considered a meritorious duty. It was the response of the faithful to the persistent call of the Qur'an to ponder creation in order to understand God's greatness. This attitude helped to cultivate an open yet inquiring bent of mind. Ancient sages were esteemed but their legacy was critically appraised. Al-Razi (d. 925), philosopher and medical scientist, while in admiration of Galen, wrote: 'But all this reverence will not and should not prevent me from doubting what is erroneous in his theories.' Ibn Haytham (Alhazen), al-Biruni and Ibn Sina (Avicenna), in challenging the long held view of Euclid and Ptolemy that the eye sent out visual rays to the object of vision, laid the foundations for modern optics.

Research was recognised as a way of intellectual growth, an ethical duty since the human intellect is a divine gift to be cherished and cultivated. 'Accept whatever adds to your wisdom, regardless of the nature of its source,' is a well-attested Prophetic tradition. 'Wisdom sustains the intellect' whose 'nateural disposition is to learn from experience,' are among the sayings of Hazrat 'Ali. Jurists and mystics, from the classical Middle Ages to the 20th century, from al-Ghazali, Ibn Khallikan and Sana'i to Shaykh Shalut and Mohammad Iqbal, have upheld and celebrated the never-ending duty of the mind to push the frontiers of its gaze to ever expanding horizons to capture glimpses of a flawless, continuing creation.

Ethic of Compassion and Sharing

A truly enlightened society urges the care of the weak and restraint in their sway by the rich and powerful. Scriptural tradition regards wealth as a blessing, and its honest creation one's duty for it can aid the general welfare of society. 'When the prayer is finished, scatter in the land and seek God's bounty, and remember God frequently; haply you will prosper.' But when misused or hoarded, wealth is a derisory pittance, an illusory source of power. The pious are the socially conscious who recognise in their wealth a right for the indigent and the deprived whom they help for the sake of God alone, without any desire for recompense or thankfulness from those whom they help.

Charity is not just sharing one's material wealth. Generosity with one's intellectual, spiritual, material or physical wherewithal is highly commended. When withheld, such gifts are a futile burden, 'a twisted collar tied to the miser's neck.' 'One who is more blessed by God,' goes an 'Alid tradition, 'is needed more for people.' The ethic of voluntary service is, thus, a strongly marked trait of Muslim tradition, celebrated in the example of the *ansar*, the Helpers, the honourable title for those citizens of Medina who gave succour to Muhammad and his fellow fugitives when they had to emigrate from Makkah to escape persecution.

Ethic of Self-reliance

The poor, the deprived and those at the margin of existence have a moral right to society's compassion, the tradition reminds frequently. But Muslim ethic discourages a culture of dependency since it undermines one's dignity, preservation of which is emphatically urged in Muslim scripture. 'Man shall have only that for which he labours,' says the Qur'an. That encouragement to self-help is reinforced in Prophetic traditions: 'Man cannot exist without constant effort.' 'The effort is from me, its fulfilment comes from God.' From the time of the Prophet, therefore, the greater emphasis of the charitable effort has been to help the needy to become self-reliant. It has been narrated, for instance, that the Prophet would rather that a mendicant was helped to equip himself for gathering and selling wood to earn sustenance. During his tenure as the last of the four rightly-guided caliphs, Hazrat 'Ali helped, for instance, to fund a self-help scheme, voluntarily proposed by a group of residents of an area, to improve its irrigation potential. He preferred that people should prosper, he explained, to their remaining economically weak.

Ethic of Respect for Life and Health Care

As the care of the poor, so that of the sick and disabled, is a frequently articulated duty. Good health, like knowledge, is a divine gift, says the Qur'an, which forcefully urges the sanctity of human life, equating the saving of one life to the saving of the entirety of humanity. 'God has sent down a treatment for every ailment,' is an oft-quoted saying of the Prophet. People achieve happiness because of the gift of reason, of which medicine is a salient fruit, so wrote a tenth-century physician al-Majusi in the introduction to his canon. Learning medicine, according to Muslim jurists, is a 'duty of sufficiency,' which is incumbent upon, not every individual, but a sufficient number of people to serve the health needs of a community. Under Muslim patronage, medicine made far reaching strides. Encyclopaedic treatises on medicine, particularly of Ibn Sina and ar-Razi enjoyed a pre-eminent status in the medical literature of learned societies as far apart as Central Asia and Europe. Hospitals flourished as did mobile dispensaries, which were, not uncommonly, staffed by both male and female health personnel.

The science of medicine was supported by meticulous research. In the late 14th century, when the great plague, the Black Death, struck Europe and Asia, Muslim physicians rejected the widely entrenched superstition that the scourge was a divine retribution. Explaining their scientific hypothesis of contagion, Ibn al-Khatib, an eminent statesman and physician of Granada, wrote that the existence of contagion was established by experience, study of the evidence of the senses, by trustworthy reports of transmission, by the spread of it by persons, by infection of a healthy sea-port by an arrival from an infected land, by the immunity of isolated individuals. 'It must be a principle that a proof taken from the tradition has to undergo modification when in manifest contradiction with the evidence of the perception of the senses.'

Ethic of Sound Mind

An equal, if not greater, emphasis was placed on mental heath since preservation of sound mind is among the foundational principles of

Islam's ethical code. The principle was seriously applied in practice. In designating a ward of the Mansuria Hospital, built in Cairo in 1284, for mental patients, its endowment deed stipulated: 'The foremost attention is to be paid to those who have suffered loss of mind and hence loss of honour.' The principle has had a wider application in tradition. Any substance abuse which interferes with the normal functioning of the mind is a greater violation of the ethical code for it amounts to self-inflicted loss of personal dignity and of the ability to fulfil one's responsibility to oneself, to one's family and to society. 'Do not be cast into ruin by your hands,' is a recurring admonition.

Ethic of Sustainable Environment: Physical, Social and Cultural

Care of the environment, in its comprehensive meaning, is a duty of trusteeship which humankind owes by virtue of its vicegerency over creation. Each generation of people are described as both 'viceroys and successors in the earth,' stewards over its resources for the benefit of all living beings. Profligacy, wastage and acts that corrupt the balanced order of nature, which is a sign of divine beneficence, earn a severe reproach. The evil that people do 'vanishes as jetsam and what profits men abides in the earth.' Hence, those who create wealth in its diverse forms, intellectual and spiritual, cultural and material, are raised to a position of honour, but only if they recognize and respect the element of trust in what they create. To squander in vanity or to withhold in jealousy what they are able to create, amounts to usurping the rights of those, including the generations yet to be born, who need the fruits of their talents. Each generation is, thus, ethic bound to leave behind a wholesome, sustainable social and physical environment.

Ethic of Governance

Those who control and administer resources for the benefit of others are bound by the duty of trusteeship. In Shi'a Islam, this duty is owed to the Imam. The Muslim tradition of religious law, thus, firmly grounds the ethic of governance in the principles of trust, probity, equity and accountability. The scripture, for instance, sternly warns corruptly inclined citizens and authorities against collusion to defraud others. Guardians of orphans and the weak are similarly warned not to compromise their fiduciary obligations, and to keep away from their wards' property 'except to improve it.' The tradition, hence, obliges administrators of a charitable foundation not only to maintain, but to seek to enhance, the value of its corpus and maximise its yield in order to sustain its charitable commitments.

Copyright The Institute of Ismaili Studies, for the Aga Khan Development Network, London, 2001. Complete text at *http: //www.iis.ac.uk/learning/life_long_learning/akdn_ethical_framework/ akdn_ethical_framework.htm*

Appendix C

Excerpts from
The Islamic Code of Medical Ethics

Adopted by the Islamic Organization for Medical Sciences (IOMS)

Contents

Introduction

First	Definition of Medical Profession
Second	Characterization of Medical Practitioner
Third	Relation between Doctor and Doctor
Fourth	Relation between Doctor and Patient
Fifth	Professional Secrecy
Sixth	Doctor's Duty in War Time
Seventh	Responsibility and Liability
Eight	The Sanctity of Human Life
Ninth	Doctor and Society
Tenth	Doctor and Biotechnological Advances
Eleventh	Medical Education
Twelfth	The Oath of the Doctor

1. Definition of Medical Profession

- The provision of medical practice is a religious dictate upon the community, *fard kifaya*, that can be satisfied on behalf of the community by some citizens taking up medicine. It is the duty of the State to ensure the needs of the nation for doctors in the various needed specialities. In Islam, this is a duty that the ruler owes the nation.

- Need may arise to import from afar such medical expertise that is not locally available. It is the duty of the State to satisfy this need.

- It also behoves the State to recruit suitable candidates from the nation's youth to be trained as doctors. An ensuing duty therefore is to establish relevant schools, faculties, clinics, hospitals and institutions that are adequately equipped and manned to fulfill that purpose.

- 'Medicine' is a religious necessity for society. In religious terms, whatever is necessary to satisfy that 'necessity' automatically acquires the status of a 'necessity'. Exceptions shall therefore be made from certain general rules of jurisprudence for the sake of making medical education possible. One such example is the intimate inspection of the human body whether alive or dead, without in any way compromising the respect befitting the human body in life and death, and always in a climate of piety and awareness of the presence of God.

- The preservation of man's life should embrace also the utmost regard to his dignity, feelings, tenderness and the privacy of his sentiments and body parts. A patient is entitled to full attention, care and feeling of security while with his doctor. The doctor's privilege of being exempted from some general rules is only coupled with more responsibility and duty that he should carry out in conscientiousness and excellence in observing God. 'Excellence that entails that you worship God as if you see Him, for even though you don't see Him, He sees you.'

Al-Ghazali considered the profession of medicine as *fardh kifaya*, a duty of society that some of its members can carry in lieu of the whole. This is natural since the need of health is a primary need and not a subsequent one. If health is seriously impaired, hardly anything in life remains enjoyable.

That it is permissible for the purpose of treatment to look at hidden and private parts of the body, derives from the rule of jurisprudence 'necessities override prohibitions'... and complies, with the Qur'anic excuse when 'compelled to do something but without ill-intention'. Since the early days of Islam the Lady-Healer's corps joined the Prophet's army to battle caring for the casualties and dressing their wounds on whatever part of the body. This provoked no dispute or divergence of opinion.

To import medical expertise and to treat Muslims by non-Muslim physicians should be decided only by the condition of the patient and the capability of the doctor.

Since an early time the Muslim state employed Christian doctors from Jundishapur and treated them very generously. In this context it is also worthy remembering that the Prophet's guide on the journey of Hijra was Abdullah ibn Uraikit, a non-Muslim, chosen by the Prophet on account of his honesty and thorough knowledge of the road.

6. Doctor's Duty in Wartime

- Since the earliest battles of Islam it was decreed that the wounded is protected by his wound and the captive by his captivity. The faithful are praised in the Qur'an as: 'they offer food – dear as it is – to the needy, orphan or captive, (saying): We feed you for the sake of God without seeking any reward or gratitude from you.' The Prophet (peace be upon him) said to his companions: 'I entrust the captives to your charity'... and they did ... even giving them priority over themselves in the best of the food they shared. It is of interest to note that this was thirteen centuries prior to the Geneva Convention and the Red Cross.
- Whatever the feelings of the doctor and wherever they lie, he shall stick to the one and only duty of protecting life and treating ailment or casualty.
- Whatever the behaviour of the enemy, the Muslim doctor shall not change his course, for each side reflects his own code of behaviour. God made it clear in the Qur'an: 'Let not the wrongdoing of others sway you into injustice.'

- As part of the international medical family, Muslim doctors should lend all support on a global scale to protect and support this noble course of the medical profession... for it is a blessing to all humanity if this humanitarian role is abided with on both sides of the battlefront.
- The medical profession shall not permit its technical, scientific or other resources to be utilized in any sort of harm or destruction or infliction upon man of physical, psychological, moral or other damage ... regardless of all political or military considerations.
- The doings of the doctor shall be unidirectional, aiming at the offering of treatment and cure to ally and enemy, be this at the personal or general level.
- The practice of medicine is lawful only to persons suitably educated, trained and qualified, fulfilling the criteria spelt out in the law. A clear guidance is the Prophet's tradition: 'Whosoever treats people without knowledge of medicine, becomes liable.'
- With the availability of medical specialization, problem cases shall be referred to the relevant specialist. 'Each one is better suited to cope with what he was meant for.'
- In managing a medical case the doctor shall do what he can to the best of his ability. If he does, without negligence, taking the measures and precautions expected from his equals, then he is not to blame or punishment even if the results were not satisfactory.
- The doctor is the patient's agent on his body. The acceptance by the patient of a doctor to treat him is considered an acceptance of any line of treatment the doctor prescribes. If treatment entails surgical interference, the initial acceptance referred to should be documented in writing, for the sake of protecting the doctor against possible eventualities. If the patient declines or refuses the doctor's prescribed plan of treatment, this refusal should also be documented by writing, witnesses or patient's signature as the situation warrants or permits.
- When fear is the obstacle preventing the patient from consent, the doctor may help his patient with a medicine such as a tranquilizer to free his patient from fear but without abolishing or suppressing his consciousness, so that the patient is able to make his choice in calmness and tranquility. By far the best method to achieve this

is the poise of the doctor himself and his personality, kindness, patience and the proper use of the spoken word.

- In situations where urgent and immediate surgical or other interference is necessary to save life, the doctor should go ahead according to the Islamic rule: 'Necessities override prohibitions.' His position shall be safe and secure whatever the result achieved, on condition that he has followed established medical methodology in a correct way. The 'bad' inherent in not saving the patient outweighs the presumptive 'good' in leaving him to his self-destructive decision. The Islamic rule proclaims that 'warding off' the 'bad' takes priority over bringing about the 'good'.

- The Prophetic guidance is 'Help your brother when he is right and when he is wrong.' When concurring with helping a brother if right but surprised at helping him when wrong, the Prophet answered his companions: 'Forbid him from being wrong ... for this is the help he is in need of.'

In conclusion, the basic religious criteria protecting the Medical Practitioner are: (1) recognized certification; (2) acceptance of the doctor by his patient; (3) good faith on part of the doctor and sole aim of curing his patient; (4) absence of unacceptable fault as defined by medical by-laws.

8. The Sanctity of Human Life

- 'On that account We decreed for the Children of Israel that whoever kills a human soul, other than for manslaughter or corruption in the land, it shall be as if he killed all mankind, and whosoever saves the life of one, it shall be as if he saved the life of all mankind' (Qur'an, 5:32).

- Human life is sacred ... and should not be wilfully taken except upon the indications specified in Islamic jurisprudence, all of which are outside the domain of the medical profession.

- A doctor shall not take away life even when motivated by mercy. This is prohibited because it is not one of the legitimate indications for killing. Direct guidance in this respect is given by the Prophet's tradition: 'In old times there was a man with an ailment that taxed his endurance. He cut his wrist with a knife and bled to death. God was displeased and said: 'My subject hastened his end ... I deny him Paradise.'

Mercy killing – like suicide – finds no support except in the atheistic way of thinking that believes that our life on this earth is followed by void. If this is sound thinking, it would have been reasonable for almost all of the human race to commit suicide and get rid of the difficulties of life... for indeed hardly a life is devoid of difficulty or pain. The claim of killing for painful hopeless illness is also refuted, for there is no human pain that cannot be conquered by medication or by suitable neurosurgery. Another category is killing to obviate the miseries presumably ensuing upon deformity. If this earns acceptance, then it will not be long until claims are made to kill the aged and unproductive members of society as a measure of combating the sequelae of population growth beyond available resources.

- The sanctity of human life covers all its stages, including intrauterine life of the embryo and foetus. This shall not be compromised by the doctor save for the absolute medical necessity recognised by Islamic jurisprudence.

This is completely in harmony with modern medical science which lately has embraced a new speciality called Fetal Medicine... striving to diagnose and treat affliction of the foetus in utero, and devise an artificial placenta to sustain foetuses aborted before viability.

Modern permissive abortion policies are not sanctioned by Islam, which accords several rights to the foetus. There is a money ransom on abortion in Islam. A foetus has rights of inheritance and if aborted alive and dies, it is inherited by its legal heirs. If a pregnant woman is sentenced to death for a crime, execution is postponed until she delivers and nurses the baby... even if that pregnancy was illegitimate. The basic right to life of the foetus is therefore self-evident.

- In his defence of life, however, the doctor is well advised to realize his limit and not transgress it. If it is scientifically certain that life cannot be restored, then it is futile to diligently keep on the vegetative state of the patient by heroic means of animation or preserve him by deep-freezing or other artificial methods. It is the process of life that the doctor aims to maintain and not the process of dying. In any case, the doctor shall not take a positive measure to terminate the patient's life.

- To declare a person dead is a grave responsibility that ultimately rests with the doctor. He shall appreciate the seriousness of his verdict and pass it in all honesty and only when sure of it. He may dispel any trace of doubt by seeking counsel and resorting to modern scientific gear.

- The doctor shall do his best that what remains of the life of an incurable patient will be spent under good care, moral support and freedom from pain and misery.

- The doctor shall comply with the patient's right to know his illness. The doctor's particular way of answering should, however, be tailored to the particular patient in question. It is the doctor's duty to thoroughly study the psychological acumen of his patient. He shall never fall short of suitable vocabulary if the situation warrants the deletion of frightening nomenclature or coinage of new names, expressions or descriptions.

- In all cases the doctor should have the ability to bolster his patients faith and endow him with tranquility and peace of mind.

10. Doctor and Bio-technological Advances

- There is no censorship in Islam on scientific research, be it academic to reveal the signs of God in His creation, or applied aiming at the solution of a particular problem.

- Freedom of scientific research shall not entail the subjugation of Man... subjecting him to definite or probable harm, withholding his therapeutic needs, defrauding him or exploiting his material need.

- Freedom of scientific research shall not entail cruelty to animals or their torture. Suitable protocols should be laid for the non-cruel handling of experimental animals during experimentation.

- The methodology of scientific research and the applications resultant thereof shall not entail the commission of sin prohibited by Islam such as fornication, confounding of genealogy, deformity or tampering with the essence of the human personality, its freedom and eligibility to bear responsibility.

- The medical profession has the right and owes the duty of effective participation in the formulation and issuing of religious verdict concerning the lawfulness or otherwise of the unprecedented outcomes of current and future advances in biological science. The verdict should be reached in togetherness between Muslim specialists in jurisprudence and Muslim specialists in biosciences. One-sided opinions have always suffered from a lack of comprehension of technical or legal aspects.
- The guiding rule in unprecedented matters falling under no extant text or law, is the Islamic dictum: 'Wherever welfare is found, there exists the statute of God.'
- The individual patient is the collective responsibility of Society that has to ensure his health needs by any means, inflicting no harm on others. This comprises the donation of body fluids or organs such as blood transfusion to the bleeding or a kidney transplant to the patient with bilateral irreparable renal damage. This is another *fard kifaya*, a duty that donors fulfill on behalf of society. Apart from the technical procedure, the onus of public education falls on the medical profession which should also draw the procedural, organizational and technical regulations and the policy of priorities.
- Organ donation shall never be the outcome of compulsion, family embarrassment, social or other pressure or exploitation of financial need.
- Donation shall entail the exposure of the donor to harm.
- The medical profession bears the greatest portion of responsibility for laying down the laws, rules and regulations organizing organ donation during life or after death by a statement in the donor's will or the consent of his family; as well as the establishment of tissue and organ banks for tissues amenable to storage. Cooperation with similar banks abroad is to be established on the basis of reciprocal aid.

Umar ibn al-Khattab, the second Caliph, decreed that if a man living in a locality died of hunger being unable of self-sustenance, then the community should pay his money ransom (*fidiah*) as if they had killed him. The similitude to people dying because of lack of blood transfusion or a donated kidney is very close.

Two traditions of the Prophet seem to be quite relevant in this respect. The one is: 'The faithful in their mutual love and compassion are like the body ... if one member complains of an ailment all other members will rally in response.' The other tradition says, 'The faithful to one another are like the blocks in a whole building ... they fortify one another.'

God described the faithful in the Qur'an saying: 'They give priority over themselves, even though they are needy.' This is even a step further than donating a kidney, for the donor can dispense with one kidney and live normally with the other... as routinely ascertained medically prior to donation.

If the living are able to donate, then the dead are even more so; and no harm will afflict the cadaver if heart, kidneys, eyes or arteries are taken to be put to good use in a living person. This is indeed a charity ... and directly fulfils God's words: 'And whosoever saves a human life, it is as though he has saved all mankind.'

A word of caution, however, is necessary. Donation should be voluntary by free will ... or the dictatorship will confiscate people's organs, thus violating two basic Islamic rights: the right of freedom and the right of ownership.

In the society of the faithful, donation should be generous supply and should be the fruit of faith and love of God and His subjects. Other societies should not beat us to this noble goal.

12. The Oath of the Doctor

I swear by God, the Great:
- To regard God in carrying out my profession;
- To protect human life in all stages and under all circumstances, doing my utmost to rescue it from death, malady, pain and anxiety;
- To keep peoples' dignity, cover their privacies and lock up their secrets;
- To be, all the way, an instrument of God's mercy, extending my medical care to near and far, virtuous and sinner, and friend and enemy;
- To strive in the pursuit of knowledge and harnessing it for the benefit but not the harm of Mankind;

- To revere my teacher, teach my junior and be brother to members of the medical profession joined in piety and charity;
- To live my faith in private and in public, avoiding whatever blemishes me in the eyes of God, His apostle and my fellow faithful;
- And may God be witness to this Oath.

Copyright the Islamic Organisation for Medical Sciences (IOMS), Kuwait, 1981. Complete text at: *http://www.islamset.com/ethics/code/index.html*

Notes

Preface

1. The painting also resists a normative stance on eschewing human and animal representation in Muslim arts: in 'drawing from scripture', it can hardly be deemed non-religious. It might be speculated that the artist avoided being too provocative by omitting formally religious symbols. However, Mughal art (like that of, *inter alia*, the Umayyads, Fatimids and Safawids) freely broke with orthodoxy on this score. See generally Sheila S. Blair and Jonathan M. Bloom, 'Art and Architecture: Themes and Variations,' pp. 215–67, in John L. Esposito, ed., *The Oxford History of Islam* (Oxford, 1999), notably at pp. 230–36.

2. One is reminded of the floating cohabitation after a shipwreck of a Bengal tiger, an orang-utan, a hyena, a zebra and a 16-year old boy with Muslim, Christian and Hindu sensibilities in Yann Martel's acclaimed recent novel, *Life of Pi* (Toronto, 2001). The experience turns out to be less harmonious than in the Ark, but becomes part of a potent meditation on the nature of ethics and religion in a fragile modern world.

3. Owen Chadwick, *The Secularization of the European Mind in the Nineteenth Century* (Cambridge, UK, 1975), p. 13.

4. Talal Asad, *Formations of the Secular: Christianity, Islam, Modernity* (Stanford, 2003), at p. 11. Asad adds: 'It would be easy to point to innumerable "secular" agents who have perpetrated acts of great cruelty. But such attempts at defending "religion" are less interesting than asking what it is we do when we assign responsibility for "violence and cruelty" to specific agents. When

118

do we look for a clear motive? When we identify an unusual outcome that seems to us to call for justification or exoneration – and therefore for moral or legal responsibility. [T]here are theories as to how this attribution should be done (the law being paradigmatic here), and it is important to understand them and the circumstances in which they are applied in the modern world. In brief, although "religious" intentions are variously distinguished from "secular" ones in different traditions, the identification of such intentions as such is especially important in what scholars call modernity for allocating moral and legal accountability.' (p. 12)

5. Most notably in *Ethics and the Limits of Philosophy* (Cambridge, MA, 1985).

6. See, for instance, Margaret Somerville, *The Ethical Canary: Science, Society and the Modern Spirit* (Toronto, 2000), which claims that a first-level inquiry as to whether something is 'inherently wrong' can be linked to a practical concept of the 'secular sacred', to enable judgment 'without necessarily having recourse to the supernatural' (pp. xi–xii). I hasten to add that what I consider the limitations of this approach do not detract from the rich insights that Somerville brings to the study of bioethics – including the methodological ones highlighted in her proposed 'Ethics Toolbox' (pp. 279–300) – which I have drawn upon in the present text.

7. Akbar Ahmed, *Islam Under Siege: Living Dangerously in a Post-Honour World* (Cambridge, UK, 2003). Ahmed situates 'honour' in group identity or *asabiyya* with its positive ethic of compassion and justice, but also its primordial communalism that sees itself threatened by globalization and liberalism, to which it may respond with violent defensiveness as 'hyper-*asabiyya*' (see especially pp. 80–90).

8. *Arabian Nights and Days: A Novel* (*Layali alf-lela*), trans. D. Johnson-Davies (New York, 1995), p. 228.

9. For a celebration of the subversive role of novels in fostering a liberating ethos in a restrictive post-Revolutionary context, see Azar Nafisi, *Reading Lolita in Tehran: A Memoir in Books* (New York, 2003). As well, in an earlier setting of radical socio-political change, see Homa Katouzian, *Sadeq Hedayat: The Life and Literature of an Iranian Writer* (London and New York, 1991).

Chapter 1: Taking Ethics Seriously: *Adab* to Zygotes

1. M. Sadri and A. Sadri, ed. and trans., *Reason, Freedom and Democracy in Islam: Essential Writings of Abdolkarim Soroush* (Oxford, 2000), p. 120.

2. Part 2, p. 7 (1843); cited in H.V. Hong and E.H. Hong, ed. and trans., *Kierkegaard's Writings* (Princeton, 1980), vol. 4, p. 90.

3. Nasir al-Din al-Tusi, *Akhlaq-i-Nasiri* (*The Nasirean Ethics*), trans. G.M. Wickens (London, 1964), 126f. Al-Tusi, the founding writer on Shi'i ethics, built in this regard and more generally upon the neo-Aristotelian work of Miskawayh: see M. Fakhry, *Ethical Theories in Islam* (Leiden, 1991), pp. 107–42, esp. p. 134. The ethical oeuvre of Immanuel Kant (1724–1804) is mainly contained in his *Foundations of the Metaphysics of Morals* (1785) – 'it is not sufficient to do that which should be morally good that it conform to the law; it must be done for the sake of the law' – and *The Critique of Practical Reason* (1787). The *Foundations* has been called 'the most significant work of philosophy after Aristotle': Williams, *Ethics and the Limits of Philosophy*, p. 55.

4. M.H. Kamali, 'Salient Features of the Shariah: Religious and Moral Dimensions and Continuity and Change,' in Esposito, ed., *The Oxford History of Islam*, pp. 130–36, which cites the Prophet's well-known pronouncement: 'When you bring a dispute to me, some of you may be more eloquent in stating your case than others. I may consequently adjudicate on the basis of what I hear. If I adjudicate in favour of someone something that belongs to his brother, let him not take it, for it would be like taking a piece of fire' (pp. 132–33).

5. Al-Tusi, *Akhlaq-i Nasiri*, p. 190. The same premise underlies the *opus* of Muslim political thought, al-Farabi's *al-Madina al-Fadila* (*The Virtuous City*): R. Walzer, *Al-Farabi on the Perfect State* (Oxford, 1985).

6. Fakhry, *Ethical Theories*, p. 12; Vincent Connell, 'From Shariah to Taqwa: Islam and Ethics,' in *The Oxford History of Islam*, pp. 96–97.

7. The Shari'a ranges over theology, rituals, ethics, law, civil behaviour and even personal hygiene, in other words, all of secular and sacred life. The *fiqh* comprises principles of jurisprudence (*usul al-fiqh*) and specific legal rules (*furu' al-fiqh*) covering public and private social regulation from constitutional to family law. See generally Fazlur Rahman, 'Law and Ethics in Islam,' in R. Hovannisian, ed., *Ethics in Islam* (Malibu, CA, 1985), pp. 3–15; M.K. Masud, 'The Scope of Pluralism in Islamic Moral Traditions,' in Sohail H. Hashmi, ed., *Islamic Political Ethics* (Princeton, 2002), pp. 135–47, notably at pp. 139–41.

8. See generally Mark Johnson, *Moral Imagination: Implications of Cognitive Science for Ethics* (Chicago, 1993), and Alasdair MacIntyre, *After Virtue: A Study in Moral Theory* (2nd ed., Notre Dame, IN, 1984).

9. See Paul Hardy, ed., *Traditions of Islam: Understanding the Hadith* (London, 2002).

10. Ira M. Lapidus, *A History of Islamic Societies* (Cambridge, UK, 2002), pp. 125–32; Fakhry, *Ethical Theories*, p. 5–6.

11. See, for example, Barbara Metcalf, *Moral Conduct and Authority: The Place of Adab in South Asian Islam* (Berkeley, CA, 1984) and especially Brian Silver, 'The Adab of Musicians,' pp. 315–29.

12. See Lapidus, *A History of Islamic Societies*, pp. 126–8; Ali S. Asani, *Ecstasy and Enlightenment: The Ismaili Devotional Literature of South Asia* (London, 2002); Aziz Esmail, *A Scent of Sandalwood: Indo-Ismaili Religious Lyrics* (London, 2002).

13. See, *inter alia*, N. Mahfouz, *The Cairo Trilogy* (*Palace Walk, Palace of Desire* and *Sugar Street*), trans. W.M. Hutchins (London, 2001); O. Pamuk, *My Name is Red*, trans. E.M. Goknar (New York, 2001); T. Salih, *The Wedding of Zein and Other Tales*, trans. D. Johnson-Davies (London, 1969); Ahdaf Soueif, *The Map of Love* (New York, 1999); and M.G. Vassanji, *The Gunny Sack* (Oxford, 1989) and *The Book of Secrets: A Novel* (Toronto, 1994). On the subversive role of literature in nurturing civic ethics, especially with regard to gender equity, see Nafisi, *Reading Lolita in Tehran: A Memoir*. On the social context in which formal and informal normative power is exercised in the contemporary Middle East and beyond, see Sami Zubaida, *Law and Power in the Islamic World* (London, 2003).

14. See Hamid Dabashi, *Close Up: Iranian Cinema* (London and New York, 2001); Richard Tapper, *The New Iranian Cinema: Politics, Representation and Identity* (London, 2002). In Jamshed Akrami's authoritative documentary film, *Friendly Persuasion: Iranian Cinema After the Revolution* (2001), Richard Pena – program director of The Film Society of Lincoln Centre, New York – describes Iranian films as presenting 'a model of intellectual cinema that one can find virtually nowhere else,' and its leading lights, notably Abbas Kiarostami and Mohsen Makhmalbaf, as among the greatest directors at work today.

15. Soroush, *Reason, Freedom, and Democracy in Islam*, pp. 105–21. By distinguishing a 'morality fit for Gods' from 'a morality fit for servants of God,' we come to terms with the 'familiar exception-bound moral rules' that offer the 'best guarantee of justice and moderation' – away from focusing exclusively on 'a higher morality' in whose name violations and deceptions abound in history (pp. 106, 116).

16. Rahman, 'Law and Ethics in Islam,' pp. 11–15 (quote at p. 11). See also K. Abou El Fadl et al., *The Place of Tolerance in Islam* (Boston, 2002); M. Arkoun, *The Unthought in Contemporary Islamic Thought* (London, 2002); E. Moosa, 'Configuring Muslim Thought,' *ISIM Newsletter* (Institute for the Study of Islam in the Modern World), 12 (2003), pp. 30–31, *www.isim.nl*.

17. Frederick M. Denny, 'Ethics and the Qur'an: Community and World View,' in *Ethics in Islam*, pp. 103–21, at p. 117.

18. McIntyre, *After Virtue*, pp. 204–25, notably at pp. 211–12.

19. Ibid., p. 216.

20. Anna Peterson, *Being Human: Ethics, Environment and Our Place in the World* (Berkeley, CA, 2001), p. 5.

21. *The Ethics of Aristotle: The Nicomachean Ethics*, trans. J.A.K. Thompson (London, 1976); see especially the Introduction by Jonathan Barnes.

22. Majid Fakhry, 'Philosophy and Theology,' in *The Oxford History of Islam*, pp. 269–303, at pp. 286–9. The ethical opus of Ibn Rushd or Averroes, the *Kitab al-akhlaq*, is no longer extant, but his Hellenic readings and recasting are replete with ethical reflections. See Ralph Lerner, *Averroes on Plato's Republic* (Ithaca, NY, 1974), and Ralph Lerner and Muhsin Mahdi, ed., *Medieval Political Philosophy: A Sourcebook* (Ithaca, NY, 1972).

23. G.B. Madison, 'The Moral-Cultural Order,' pp. 38–74, *The Political Economy of Civil Society and Human Rights* (London and New York, 1998), at p. 62.

24. As proposed in the leading liberal model of distributive justice by John Rawls, *A Theory of Justice* (Cambridge, MA, 1971).

25. Ronald Dworkin, *Sovereign Virtue: The Theory and Practice of Equality* (Cambridge, MA, 2000), pp. 249–54, 275–76; see also more generally at 211–36. Dworkin ultimately ties his liberalism – in which justice and equality are primary – to a critical morality that he calls 'ethical individualism', in which the first principle is of 'objective' human value shared universally, and the second of 'special responsibility' apropos each individual life (pp. 446–52). But rather than adding to the earlier picture of performative competence as the criterion of the 'good,' this only leads him to give a more detailed account of fairness in resource distribution by society for the benefit of every citizen. At the same time, Dworkin is clearly concerned about the intertwining of individual and communal ethics, as noted elsewhere in this study.

26. Williams, *Ethics and the Limits of Philosophy*, pp. 197–8, 200 (quote at p. 200). He adds: '[A] dream of a community of reason ... is far too removed, as Hegel first said it was, from social and historical reality and from any concrete sense of a particular ethical life – farther removed from those things, in some ways, than the religion it replaced. These various versions of moral philosophy share a false image of how reflection is related to practice, an image of theories in terms of which they uselessly elaborate their differences from one another.'

27. Ibid., p. 201.

28. J. Habermas, *The Future of Human Nature* (Cambridge, UK, 2003), pp. 2–5 (quote at p. 4).

29. Ibid.: 'moral theory ... dissolves the context that first linked moral judgements with the motivation toward right action.'

30. Williams, *Ethics and the Limits of Philosophy*, pp. 182–96, notably, at pp. 188–89.

31. See generally Peter Singer, 'Introduction,' in P. Singer, ed., *Ethics*, (New York and Oxford, 1994), pp. 4–5; Williams, pp. 6–11; Habermas, pp. 32–7. For Williams, a major problem with the contemporary understanding of morality is that it is irredeemably attached to obligation; he therefore prefers to treat 'moral philosophy' as ethics.

32. Habermas, pp. 32–34, 39–40. '[T]he abstract morality of reason proper to subjects of human rights is itself sustained by a prior *ethical self-understanding of the species*, which is shared by all *moral persons*' (pp. 32, 40).

33. Kant, *Foundations*, note 3, *supra*.

34. See especially Williams, pp. 175–96, and Habermas, pp. 7–11, 37.

35. To quote Sohail Hashmi's preface *in Islamic Political Ethics, supra* note 6, p. xii.

36. Søren Kierkegaard, *Journals and Papers* (1843), vol. 1. For a succinctly trenchant set of reflections on the interplay of 'history' and 'transcendence' on this score, see Ebrahim Moosa, 'Configuring Muslim Thought,' *supra* note 16.

37. See John Caiazza, 'The Arrival of Techno-Secularism,' *Modern Age*, 44: 3 (2002), pp. 208–16. Caiazza argues that it is the ubiquity of technology, not the power of scientific argument, that signals a new state of affairs: 'Technological effects have acquired a life of their own, achieving a level of change so that now technology possesses its own ethics, theology and unanticipated consequences.' (p. 214)

38. Rahman, 'Law and Ethics in Islam,' pp. 11–12.

39. A. Dallal, 'Science, Medicine, and Technology: The Making of a Scientific Culture,' *The Oxford History of Islam*, pp. 155–213, at p. 157. See more generally Max Meyerhof, *Studies in Medieval Arabic Medicine: Theory and Practice*, ed. P. Johnstone (London, 1984).

40. Dallal, pp. 205–7. The historical record now establishes al-Nafis's discovery of pulmonary blood circulation well before the standard attribution to William Harvey (1578–1657), as well as the impact in Europe of al-Nafis's incisive *Commentary* (among other works) on Ibn Sina's 10th century *Canon of Medicine*. Al-Baghdadi conducted an immense sampling of skeletal remains from a famine that struck Egypt in 1200, and used his findings to correct

Galen's descriptions of the lower jaw and sacrum; he ensured 'objectivity' by arranging for independent bone appraisals.

41. Ibid., 207–10; V. Rispler-Chaim, *Islamic Medical Ethics in the Twentieth Century* (Leiden, 1993), p. 2 (including historical citations), where the prolific medieval works are contrasted with the dearth in contemporary Muslim bioethical literature.

42. Dallal appears to straddle these two readings. On the one hand, he asserts that 'science was considered a value-free undertaking that needed no religious or ethical justification,' for the religious discourse effectively separated the two enterprises. Yet he also observes that the locus of science and its practitioners was within the mainstream institutions of society, wherein men of science were also jurists and timekeepers in mosques. (pp. 212–13). It is surely ahistorical to insist that Muslim science was a 'secular enterprise,' when the separation of those universes only came about with the Enlightenment.

43. A modern version of the 'Islamized' Hippocratic Oath appears in '*The Islamic Code of Medical Ethics*,' Appendix C below.

44. Even in the modern period, sustained rationales for postmortem examinations as part of a physician's training to acquire clinical competence in serving society, and for humane justice, was required by the leading Egyptian jurists Rashid Rida and Husnayn Makhluf: see Rispler-Chaim, pp. 72–8. The *Islamic Code of Medical Ethics* is clearly sensitive to this concern: see section 6 thereof (Appendix C). On *maslaha* generally, see M.K. Masud, *Shatibi's Philosophy of Islamic Law* (Islamabad, 1995), which highlights the role of public interest elements in the mutability of the Shari'a and *fiqh* in the hands of a remarkable 14th century jurist.

45. A genome is an individual's entire genetic composition, the full set of DNA carried within one's genes. Some 30–40,000 genes are contained within the genome. As such, it is what makes one a human. The Human Genome Project was begun in 1990, to map the overall sequence of every gene within the genome as a shared public project with research teams in some 20 countries. See H. Thorsteinsdóttir et al., 'Genomics Knowledge,' in Richard Smith et al., ed., *Global Public Goods for Health* (New York, 2003), pp.137–58. See also the World Health Organization (WHO)'s Genome Resource Centre, which includes emerging ethical and social perspectives on genomic technologies: *http://www.who.int/genomics/en/*.

46. Quoted in Francis Fukuyama, *Our Posthuman Future: Consequences of the Biotechnology Revolution* (New York, 2002), p. 18. Haseltine heads the private corporation Human Genome Science. Likewise, many of the biotech-

boosters in Stephen S. Hall, *Merchants of Immortality: Chasing the Dream of Human Life Extension* (New York, 2003) appear to regard any ethical opposition to exploiting 'biomedical opportunities' as inspired by nothing more than speculation and ideology.

47. Fukuyama, a member of the President's Council on Bioethics in the U.S., notes that the Human Genome Project allocated three per cent of its budget at the outset to studying the ethical and socio-legal implications of genetic research, which may reflect 'commendable concern' or be regarded as 'protection money the scientists have to pay' against 'true ethicists'. He contrasts the latter with professional bioethicists subject to 'regulatory capture' whereby they serve as rationalizing agents for the industry that pays them. *Our Posthuman Future*, p. 204.

48. See T. Beauchamp, 'The Four Principles Approach,' pp. 3–12; G. Serour, 'Islam and the Four Principles,' pp. 75–92; K. Hasan, 'Islam and the Four Principles: A Pakistan View,' pp. 93–103, in R. Gillon, ed., *Principles of Health Care Ethics* (New York, 1994). The classic text on the subject is by T.L. Beauchamp and J.L. Childress, *Principles of Biomedical Ethics* (5th ed., New York, 1991).

49. Daniel Patrick Moynihan, the late New York senator, quoted in Michael Lacey, '"Catholicism and American Freedom": That Old-World Religion,' The *New York Times Review of Books* (3 August 2003); *http://www.nytimes.com/ 2003/08/03/books/review/03LACEY.html*.

50. A distinction that is discussed in the next essay of this study.

51. See Rispler-Chaim, *Islamic Medical Ethics*, pp. 7–18; more generally, see D.C. Maguire, *Sacred Choices: The Right to Contraception and Abortion in Ten World Religions* (Minneapolis, MN, 2001), especially at p. 107.

52. Rispler-Chaim, *Islamic Medical Ethics*, pp. 8–9, citing an assortment of *fatwas* (religio-legal edicts). An abortion after the 120-day phase is deemed a crime against a person. For a view that holds the Qur'an is 'silent' on the point of ensoulment, see A. Sachedina, 'Islamic perspectives on cloning,' at *http://www.people.virginia.edu/~aas/issues/cloning.htm*.

53. A normative injunction holds, for example, that a pregnant woman may not be executed at any point before delivery: see the *Islamic Code of Medical Ethics*, in Appendix C, section 8.

54. Most notably the then Sheikh of Al-Azhar, the principle legal authority in Sunni Islam: *Al-Fatawa Islamiyya*, 9 (1983), cited in Rispler-Chaim, p. 11. See generally Basim F. Mussallam, 'Why Islam Permitted Birth Control,' *Arab Studies Quarterly*, 2 (1981), pp. 181–97. *The Islamic Code* appears more restrictive about carrying out abortions than is generally the norm, possibly

for reasons of concern about the abuse of abortion procedures on the part of physicians and patients.

55. Somerville, *The Ethical Canary: Science. Society and the Human Spirit*, pp. 26–8 (quote at p. 28).

56. I. Wilmut et al., 'Viable Offspring Derived from Fetal and Adult Mammalian Cells,' 385 *Nature* (1997), p. 810. Dolly was born in July 1996, but the story only became public with the publication of Dr. Wilmut's paper in February 1997. Cloning involves making an identical/near identical genetic copy of a cell, molecule or embryo.

57. G. Kolata, 'First mammal clone dies; Dolly made science history,' *The New York Times* (15 February 2003): *http://www.nytimes.com/2003/02/15/science/15DOLL.html.*

58. Ibid.

59. See A.S. Daar and L. Sheremata, 'The Science of Stem Cells: Some Implications for Law and Policy,' pp. 5–13, and L. Shanner, 'Stem Cell Terminology: Practical, Theological and Ethical Implications,' pp. 62–66, *Health Law Review Papers – Symposium of September 21, 2002* (University of Alberta Stem Cell Task Force): *http://www.stemcellnetwork.ca/news/features/billc13/hlr.php.* A general primer on stem cells, with updates on research developments, is offered by the U.S. National Institutes for Health (NIH) at *http://stemcells.nih.gov/index.asp.*

60. This involves inserting the nucleus of a somatic or non-reproducing cell into an enucleated egg – Somatic Cell Nuclear Transplant or SCNT – which generates a zygote and then an embryo. See the interactive primer on the nature of SCNT from *The Guardian* (UK) at *http://www.guardian.co.uk/flash/0,5860,534450,00.html.*

61. After 328 failed attempts at cloning embryos by the SCNT process, the first successful horse clone was born in May 2003. Other successful clones since 1997, again after high embryo failure rates, have yielded cats, cows, goats, mice, mules and pigs. See F. Walsh, 'First cloned horse unveiled in Italy,' *BBC World News* (6 August 2003): *http://news.bbc.co.uk/go/pr/fr/-/2/hi/science/nature/3129441.stm.* The consistent inability to clone primates has led some scientists to conclude that inherent obstacles related to the distribution of DNA in cell division at the embryonic stage will never allow human cloning: see 'Human cloning flawed,' *BBC World News* (10 April 2003): *http://news.bbc.co.uk/go/pr/fr/-/2/hi/science/nature/2936401.stm.* However, in what is regarded as a remarkable breakthrough, human embryos were successfully reported to have been created in early 2004 by SCNT and stem cells extracted from them in a South Korean laboratory. Drs Woo Suk Hwang

and Shing Yon Moon, who lead the work, insisted it was not their purpose to clone humans but to facilitate theraputic applications; the embryos were not mplanted. See G. Kolata, 'Cloning Creates Human Embryos,' *The New York Times* (12 February 2004).

62. The first US research institute to commit itself publicly to creating human embryos solely for harvesting stem cells announced shortly thereafter that it would cease the practice: 'Institute ending stem cell production,' *The New York Times* (18 January 2002), p. A19. In Canada, the *Assisted Human Reproduction and Related Research Act* of 2004 imposes a regulatory regime over the creation and use of human embryos in procedures deemed 'ethically unacceptable.' See, generally, Daar and Sheremata, 'The Science of Stem Cells,' p. 6; Somerville, *The Ethical Canary*, pp. 55–88. It should also be noted that reproductive intervention in the form of in vitro culturing for infertile couples is subject to constraints in many quarters about the sperm/egg donors being the legal parents, since third party donors render the act one of adultery. See Thomas Eich, 'Muslim Voices on Cloning,' *ISIM Newsletter*, 12 (2003), pp. 38–9.

63. Carolyn Abraham, 'Stem-cell study to begin soon in Saudi Arabia,' *The Globe and Mail* (13 June 2002), p. A7. Whether leftover embryos from the country's many fertility clinics can be used to draw stem cells was yet to be determined. However, the idea of human cloning is widely disapproved of: see A. Sachedina, 'Islamic perspectives on cloning,': *http: //www.people.virginia.edu/~aas/issues/cloning.htm*.

64. See Shanner, 'Stem Cell Terminology,' p. 65, arguing that the term 'non-reproductive' cloning is hence more appropriate than 'therapeutic'.

65. Dworkin, *Sovereign Virtue*, pp. 436–42.

66. Habermas, *The Future of Human Nature*, in terms respectively of Kierkegaard's and Kant's imperatives: pp. 5–15, 54–60. Ironically, the essential rationale for such interventions turns on the enlargement of freedom, by extending the range of choices on the parts of patients, parents, consumers and entrepreneurs.

67. Fukuyama, *Our Posthuman Future*, pp. 216–18. See also Michael Sandel, 'The Case Against Perfection,' *The Atlantic Monthly*, vol. 293:3 (2004), pp. 50–62, arguing that genetic manipulation impacts 'three key features of our moral landscape: humility, responsibility and solidarity.'

68. See the deliberations of the Islamic Organization on Medical Sciences (IOMC) in the wake of the Dolly episode and the spectre of human cloning: *http://www.islamset.com/healnews/cloning/index.html*; and the provisions on biotechnology in the IOMC's *Islamic Code of Medical Ethics*, in Appendix C .

See also A. Sachedina, 'Islamic Perspectives on Research with Human Embryonic Stem Cells,' in National Bioethics Advisory Commission, *Ethical Issues in Human Stem Cell Research: Religious Perspectives*, vol. 3 (Rockville, MD, 2000), G1–G6; and Ebrahim Moosa, 'Muslims Ask: Does Cloning Distort Creation?, *Voices Across Boundaries* (Canada), vol.1:2 (2003–4), pp. 34–37.

69. See Rispler-Chaim, *Islamic Medical Ethics*, pp. 94–99, notably at p. 97; Jalaluddin Umri, 'Suicide or Termination of Life,' trans. S.A.H. Rizvi, *Islamic and Comparative Law Quarterly* (1987), pp. 136–44.

70. Qur'anic injunctions against killing are less pointedly aimed at suicide: see Masud, 'The Scope of Pluralism in Muslim Moral Traditions,' p. 143.

71. See especially Somerville, *The Ethical Canary*, pp. 138–45.

72. Ibid., pp. 117–51, for a useful elucidation. See further the discussion of clinical and moral issues on hand in Thomas Mappes and Jane Zembaty, ed., *Biomedical Ethics* (3rd ed., New York, 1991), Chapter 7 ('Euthanasia and the Definition of Death'), especially at pp. 367–81.

73. See A.M. Clarfield, M. Gordon, M.H. Markwell and S. Alibhai, 'Ethical Issues in End-of-Life Geriatric Care: The Approach of Three Monotheistic Religions–Judaism, Catholicism, and Islam,' *Journal of the American Geriatric Society*, 51:8 (2003), pp. 1149–54, notably at p. 1152.

74. The *Code* imposes heavy obligations on the part of the physician to communicate effectively with the patient, and to relieve distress and maximize comfort, yet makes no clear reference to requiring the patient's consent to treatment, and even empowers the physician to override it in cases of 'necessity'. Indeed, the section on the physician's responsibility in wartime makes him the 'patient's agent in body'.

75. Informed consent and patient autonomy are vital aspects of the bioethics curriculum at the Aga Khan University Hospital in Karachi, Pakistan (where it is a mandatory part of its residency training programme), pointing to the diversity in Muslim perspectives: *http://www.aku.edu/bioethics/bc.PDF*. As well, the emphasis on truth-telling and disclosure in Islam weighs in favour of patient autonomy and informed consent: see Clarfield et al., 'Ethical Issues in End-of-Life Geriatric Care,' at pp. 1152–53.

76. Somerville, *The Ethical Canary*, p. 129. At this point, the only country to take a legally permissive position on euthanasia is the Netherlands; the U.S. state of Oregon also has permissive legislation for physicians.

77. See generally H.A. Shenkin, *Medical Ethics: Evolution, Rights and the Physician* (Dordrecht and Boston, 1991), especially at p. 354.

78. See *The Islamic Code*, Appendix C, section 10.

79. Rispler-Chaim, *Islamic Medical Ethics*, p. 30.

80. A resistance that also stems from the Shari'a principle that burial ought to occur promptly after death, for the sake of spiritual proximity to the Creator and all that is in store for the soul.

81. Thus, *The Islamic Code* (section 10) urges voluntary donations after death as all the more necessary in fulfilling the ethic of charity, in giving sustenance to the living.

82. James Meek, 'Cloned pigs promise transplants to humans,' *The Guardian* (3 January 2002), p. 1.

83. See A.S. Daar, 'Xenotransplantation and religion: The major monotheistic religions,' *Xeno*, 2 (1994), pp. 61–4 (also argues that the normative prohibition does not extend beyond consuming the flesh).

84. See especially Somerville, *The Ethical Canary*, pp. 98–116, drawing on her experience as co-chair of the National Forum on Xenotransplantation: Clinical, Ethical and Regulatory Issues,' sponsored by Health Canada in 1997. See also J.B. Dossetor and A.S. Daar, 'Ethics in Transplantation: Allotransplantation and Xenotransplantation,' in *Kidney Transplantation: Principles and Practice*, ed., P.J. Morris (5th ed., Philadelphia, 2001), pp. 732–44, notably at pp. 739–40; A.S. Daar and L.E. Chapman, 'Xenotransplantation,' in *Encyclopedia of Bioethics* (3rd ed., New York, 2003).

85. Discussed further in this and a subsequent essay in the present study.

86. Somerville observes (pp. 104–5) that the recent infectious hazards of BSE ('Mad Cow' disease) and variant Creutzfeld-Jakob disease (vCJD) have stemmed merely from cross-species consumption (cattle eating the offal of sheep), which arguably pales against the potential risk of infection in genetic crossing. Dossetor and Daar note the 'considerable evidence that human immunodefiency virus (HIV) jumped species from nonhuman primates to animals' (p. 740).

87. See Margaret Visser, *Beyond Fate: The 2002 Massey Lectures* (Toronto, 2002), pp. 117–23. Genetics is first dislocated from its wider sociobiological context and given primacy, Visser argues, then used to rationalize prejudice about race, gender and whatever else comes in the way of this deterministic view of the universe. Yet 'we are far closer to predicting somebody's fate if we know her postal code than if we map her genes' (p. 122). See also Margaret Atwood's haunting sketch of a genetically manipulated universe of Orwellian proportions in her acclaimed novel, *Oryx and Crake* (Toronto, 2003).

88. The example used here is analogous to one first proposed by the philosopher Michael Stocker and cited in James Rachels, 'The Ethics of Virtue

and the Ethics of Right Action,' in *Elements of Moral Philosophy* (New York, 1978), pp. 159–79.

89. MacIntyre, *After Virtue, supra* note 18 and text thereto.

90. The esotericism of Ibn 'Arabi (1165–1240) had a pluralist tenor that earned him a following among communities from Andalusia to South Asia: see Lapidus, *A History of Islamic Societies*, pp. 173–74, 366.

91. Lapidus, *A History of Islamic Societies*, pp. 133–55.

92. S. Nomanul Haq, 'Islam and Ecology: Toward Retrieval and Reconstruction,' *Daedalus* (American Academy of Arts and Sciences), Special Issue – 'Religion and Ecology: Can the Climate Change?,' 130 (2001), pp. 141–78, at p. 153–4 (endnotes omitted); *http://www.daedalus.amacad.org/issues/fall2001/haq.htm.* See also Seyyed Hossein Nasr, 'Islam and the Environmental Crisis,' in S. Rockefeller and J. Elder, ed., *Spirit and Nature: Why the Environment Is a Religious Issue* (Boston, 1992), pp. 83–108, and his *The Encounter of Man and Nature* (London, 1978).

93. See Mawil Y.I. Deen, 'Islamic Environmental Ethics,' in J.R. Engel and J.G. Engel, ed., *Ethics of Environment and Development: Global Challenge, International Response* (Tucson, AZ, 1990), pp. 189–98, at p. 196, noting also that wildlife protection in Saudi Arabia relies on *hima*, as do Bedouin customary practices to this day.

94. Or as Baird Callicott observes, stewardship offers a meaningful response to the problem of 'moral asymmetry' in which human uniqueness does not warrant superiority: *Earth's Insights* (Berkeley and Los Angeles, 1994), pp. 21–22, cited in Peterson, *Being Human, supra* note 20, p. 219. See also O.P. Dwivedi, 'Satyagraha for conservation,' in *Ethics of Environment and Development*, pp. 201–12.

95. Haq, 'Islam and Ecology,' pp. 170–71.

96. Indeed, upon being seen wiping the mouth of his horse with a personal cloth, the Prophet explained, 'Last night I was rebuked for not looking after my horse': hadith report of Malik ibn Anas, cited in Haq, p. 169.

97. Peterson, *Being Human*, pp. 215–39. See also Rockefeller and Elder, ed., *Spirit and Nature, supra*; George Rupp, 'Religion, Modern Secular Culture, and Ecology,' pp. 23–30, and other reflections in *Daedalus*, Special Issue, *supra*.

98. See especially the sobering analysis by the Nobel-laureate Joseph E. Stiglitz, *Globalization and its Discontents* (London and New York, 2002).

99. However, contemporary Christian discourse increasingly conceives of dominion in terms of stewardship. See, for example, Loren Wilkinson, ed., *Earthkeeping in the Nineties: Stewardship of Creation* (Grand Rapids, MI,

1991), pp. 275–325; Peter De Vos, et al., *Earthkeeping: Christian Stewardship of Natural Resources* (Grand Rapids, MI, 1980), pp. 207–38.

100. See *http://www.akdn.org/*; the full text of the *Ethical Framework* is at *http://www.iis.ac.uk/learning/life_long_learning/akdn_ethical_framework/ akdn_ethical_framework.htm*.

101. Shirin Akiner, 'Prospects for Civil Society in Tajikistan', in Amyn B. Sajoo, ed., *Civil Society in the Muslim World* (London, 2002), pp. 149–93, at pp. 180–81. See also Stephen Anderson, ed., *Improving Schools Through Teacher Development: Case Studies of the Aga Khan Foundation Projects in East Africa* (Lisse, Netherlands, 2002).

102. It is noteworthy that, in the wake of the furore over the accounting practices of major corporations in the U.S., the Chairman of the U.S Securities and Exchange Commission (SEC) has called for a culture respectful of 'moral DNA' beyond the 'trap of mere compliance' with laws. See '"Put ethics first" SEC chief urges,' *The Gazette* (Montreal), (10 May 2003), p. B11.

103. Derived from the scriptural norm that transgressing 'the bounds' ultimately amounts to a wrong against oneself (Qur'an, 65:1, 16:33). See generally George Hourani, *Reason and Tradition in Islamic Ethics* (Cambridge, 1985).

Chapter 2: Civility and its Discontents

1. See A. Seligman, *The Idea of Civil Society* (New York, 1992). The opposition of 'secular' and 'religious' is of growing importance in emerging Muslim discourses. Real and imagined polarities on this score are sketched in B. Tibi, *Islam between Culture and Politics* (New York, 2001), pp. 106–15; A. Filali-Ansary, 'The Challenge of Secularization,' *Journal of Democracy*, 7 (1996), pp. 76–80; and John Keane, 'The limits of secularism,' *The Times Literary Supplement* (9 January 1998), pp. 12–13.

2. See generally F. Halliday, *Two Hours That Shook the World–September 11, 2001: Causes and Consequences* (London, 2002). For a set of insightful reflections on a renewed intellectualism, see 'What is Liberal Islam?,' *Journal of Democracy*, 14:2 (2003), pp.18–49 (featuring contributions by A. Filali-Ansary, Laith Kubba, Radwan Masmoudi and Abdelwahab El-Affendi).

3. See my cautionary comment on this score, 'Muslims beware' (Op-ed article), *The Guardian* (London), (14 September 2001), p. 22; and also prior to the events of September 11, with regard to the use of religious rhetoric in political conflicts, 'No ticket to paradise' (Op-ed article), *The Guardian* (4 September 2001), p. 16. Human rights organizations such as Amnesty International (London) and Human Rights Watch (New York) have repeatedly

warned of the grave perils of the ensuing 'war on terrorism,' and even a U.S. Government report chronicles a civil rights backlash against Muslim/Arab-Americans in the conduct of federal institutions: P. Shenon, 'Report on USA Patriot Act Alleges Civil Rights Violations,' *New York Times* (20 July 2003); *http://www.nytimes.com/2003/07/21/politics/21JUST.html?hp*. The then United Nations Human Rights Commissioner, Mary Robinson, noted on inaugurating the Commission's 58th Session in Geneva that 'we need to respond to terrorism not only by legislative and security measures but with the armory of common values, common standards and common commitments on universal rights that define us as one global community and which enable us to reach beyond our differences' (18 March 2002).

4. On the 'Constitution of Medina' see R.N. Bellah, ed., *Beyond Belief: Essays on Religion in a Post-Traditionalist World* (Berkeley, CA, 1991), especially at pp. 150–51; on al-Farabi's *al-Madina al-Fadila* see Walzer, *Al-Farabi on the Perfect State*; on Ibn Rushd see Lerner, *Averroes on Plato's Republic*. These imagined 'ethical cities', including the more esoteric one of al-Hamid al-Kirmani (d.1020) in his *Rahat al-'Aql* (*The Comfort of Reason*), drew upon Hellenistic currents and in turn influenced the Renaissance utopias of Thomas More and others. See generally Fakhry, *Ethical Theories in Islam*; Hovannisian, ed., *Ethics in Islam*; Ralph Lerner and Muhsin Mahdi, ed., *Medieval Islam Political Thought: A Sourcebook* (Ithaca, NY, 1972).

5. See J. Habermas, 'Civil Society and the Political Public Sphere,' in *Between Facts and Norms: Contributions to a Discourse Theory of Law and Democracy*, trans. W. Rehg (Cambridge, MA and Cambridge, UK, 1996), pp. 329–87; Taylor, 'The Public Sphere,' in *Philosophical Arguments*, pp. 257–87. Both are discussed in my comments on the public sphere in the Introduction to this volume.

6. See Edward Shils, 'The Virtue of Civil Society,' in *Government and Opposition*, lecture delivered at the Athenaeum Club (22 January 1991), at pp. 11–12; reprinted in V.A. Hodgkinson and M. Foley, ed., *The Civil Society Reader* (Hanover and London, 2003), pp. 292–305, notably at p. 301. In effect, Shils observes, civility 'protects liberal democratic society from the danger of extremes of partisanship it, itself, generates'.

7. The terms 'ethics' and 'morals' and their nexus are discussed at some length in the opening essay of this study.

8. C. Taylor, 'Cross-Purposes: The Liberal-Communitarian Debate,' in *Philosophical Arguments*, at p. 186.

9. Ibid., at p. 194. Taylor observes that in a broad sense, the 'right' may include 'the shared good'. But strictly speaking, a liberal consensus among

citizens in increasingly pluralist societies is about such shared goods as individual dignity and sanctity, and respect for the rule of law, in other words, values that maintain social harmony. See also his *The Ethics of Authenticity* (Cambridge, MA, 1992), in which the collective and individual good are seen as casualties of the liberal quest for 'authentic' self-fulfilment, and most recently, his *Varieties of Religion Today* (London and Cambridge, MA, 2002), on the frame of 'expressive individualism' that even shapes non-secular quests in the public sphere (Chapter 3).

10. Hence 'virtue' is 'human excellence', which requires man to 'perform his function well': *The Ethics of Aristotle: The Nicomachean Ethics*, trans. Thompson, p. 99–100, and Jonathan Barnes' Introduction to the same volume, especially pp. 29–36.

11. A.B. Seligman, 'Animadversions Upon Civil Society and Civic Virtue in the Last Decade of the Twentieth Century', in J.A. Hall, ed., *Civil Society: Theory, History, Comparison* (Cambridge, MA and Cambridge, UK, 1995), pp. 200–23, at p. 206.

12. R. Rorty, 'The Priority of Democracy to Philosophy', in *Objectivity, Relativism, and Truth: Philosophical Papers* (Cambridge, 1991), vol. 1, p. 176. He therefore advocates working for a 'post-Philosophical culture' in the name of civic pluralism. See further the critical analysis of Rorty in Keane, *Civil Society*, at pp. 57–63.

13. See Isaiah Berlin, *Four Essays on Liberty* (London, 1969), and *The Sense of Reality: Studies in Ideas and their History* (London, 1996); Karl Popper, *The Open Society and Its Enemies*, vol. 1 (London, 1945; repr., 1999).

14. Notably the 'international bill of rights' that comprises the Universal Declaration of Human Rights of 1948, and the ensuing United Nations covenants on Civil and Political Rights, and on Social, Economic and Cultural Rights. See generally C. Hesse and R. Post, ed., *Human Rights and Political Transitions: Gettysburg to Bosnia* (New York, 1999); P. Sieghart, *The Lawful Rights of Mankind: An Introduction to the International Legal Code of Human Rights* (Oxford and London, 1985); C. Taylor, *Sources of the Self: The Making of Modern Identity* (Cambridge, MA, 1989).

15. See V. Havel, *The Power of the Powerless: Citizens against the State in Central-Eastern Europe*, ed. J. Keane (New York, 1985), and *Summer Meditations*, trans. Paul Wilson (New York, 1992); John Keane, ed. *Civil Society and the State: New European Perspectives* (New York and London, 1988); Eric Gellner, *Conditions of Liberty* (London, 1994). Popper's influence on Soros is reflected in the latter's flagship Open Society Institute, which has offices across eastern and central Europe to fund civic projects.

16. R.D. Putnam, *Bowling Alone: The Collapse and Revival of American Community* (New York, 2000). The transition from essay to book is narrated at pp. 505–13. See also M. Barone's review of the book, 'Doing your own thing by yourself,' *Times Literary Supplement* (23 February 2001), p. 5.

17. Putnam, *Bowling Alone*, chapters 4, 7 and 8.

18. J.R. Saul, *On Equilibrium* (Toronto, New York, London, 2001), p. 86. Interestingly, this does not prevent him from invoking Solon, one of Athenian democracy's founding fathers, who warned of the 'public evil' that 'enters the house of each man,' past courtyards and high walls. This leads Saul to conclude that 'ethics is a public matter' (pp. 65–67) – yet he appears to see no contradiction in opposing public evil with an amoral public ethics. It is also noteworthy that 'public reason' as conceived by one of the twentieth century's leading political philosophers, John Rawls, is premised on liberal foundations that begrudge a morality linked to religious faith: see P. Berkowitz, 'John Rawls and the Liberal Faith,' *The Wilson Quarterly* (Spring 2002), pp. 60–69 (arguing that the Kantian basis of liberalism warrants a more generous acknowledgement of the intertwining of secular and sacred).

19. J. Smith, *Moralities: Sex, Money and Power in the Twenty-first Century* (London, 2001).

20. Ibid., pp. 67–148.

21. Ibid., pp. 149–86.

22. Taylor, 'The Public Sphere,' at pp. 266–71; Gellner, *Conditions of Liberty*, pp. 44–52. Richard John Neuhaus famously decried this state of affairs in *The Naked Public Square: Religion and Democracy in America* (Grand Rapids, MI, 1984); see also R. Thiemann, *Religion in Public Life: A Dilemma for Democracy* (Washington DC, 1996); S. Carter, *Civility* (New York and London, 1999), and *The Culture of Disbelief: How American Law and Politics Trivilizes Religious Devotion* (New York, 1993).

23. See, *inter alia*, A. Etzioni, *The Spirit of Community* (New York, 1994) and 'Law in Civil Society, Good Society, and the Prescriptive State,' *Chicago-Kent Law Review*, 75 (2000), p. 355; A. Giddens, ed., *The Global Third Way Debate* (Cambridge, 2001); J. Gray, *Enlightenment's Wake* (New York and London, 1995); G. Himmelfarb, *The De-Moralization of Society: From Victorian Virtues to Modern Values* (New York, 1995); R. Kuttner, *Everything is for Sale: The Virtues and Limits of Markets* (New York, 1997); M. Sandel, *Liberalism and the Limits of Justice* (Cambridge, 1998).

24. Samuel P. Huntington, *The Clash of Civilizations and the Remaking of World Order* (New York, 1996). Huntington's deterministic views about

Islam and other civilizations in the context of contemporary politics are not unique: see, for example, Lucian Pye, *Asian Power and Politics: The Cultural Dimensions of Authority* (Cambridge, MA, 1985).

25. I have critiqued these views in 'The Crescent in the Public Square,' *Islam in America*, 3 (1997), p. 1, and 'The Islamic Ethos and the Spirit of Humanism,' *International Journal of Politics, Culture and Society*, 8 (1995), p. 579. See further B.S. Turner, *Orientalism, Post-modernism and Globalism* (London and New York, 1994), especially at pp. 20–35; S.-E. Ibrahim, 'Civil Society and Prospects of Democratization in the Arab World,' in A.R. Norton, ed., *Civil Society in the Middle East* (Leiden and New York, 1995), vol. 1, p. 27.

26. See, for example, J. Clark, 'Americans are blind to barbarians at their gates' (Op-Ed), *The Times* (London), (15 September 2001), p. 18. Clark, who is Hall Professor of History at the University of Kansas, invokes Huntington in support of an all out 'jihad' against terrorism in the wake of the September events. Again, Francis Fukuyama's critique of Huntington only reinforces the 'liberal' polarizations on hand: 'The West has won,' *The Guardian* (11 October 2001), p. 21.

27. Etzioni, 'Law in Civil Society.' See also McClain and Fleming, 'Some Questions for Civil Society-Revivalists,' especially at pp. 302–9. On the idea of the Good Society, see R. Dagger, *Civic Virtues: Rights, Citizenship, and Republican Liberalism* (Oxford and New York, 1997); R.N. Bellah, R. Madsen and W.M. Sullivan, *The Good Society* (repr., New York, 1992).

28. For an eloquent exposition on this parting of the ways in liberal discourse, see Seligman, 'Civil Society and Civic Virtue,' and his *The Idea of Civil Society*.

29. Indeed, the communitarian movement has been accused of creating self-contained, exclusivist groups whose adherents have 'a long tradition of self-reliance and individualism' and undercut civic capital: see Eva Cox, *A Truly Civil Society* (Sydney, 2001), pp. 29–37, quote at p. 36. For Mary Ann Glendon, the virtue-value dichotomy and the primacy of individual liberties have eroded the 'seedbeds of virtue' in which the entire civil society project must be grounded: 'Introduction: Forgotten Questions,' in M. Glendon and D. Blankenhorn, ed., *Seedbeds of Virtue: Sources of Competence, Character, and Citizenship in American Society* (Lanham, Madison, 1995), p. 1, especially at p. 12.

30. Gellner, *Conditions of Liberty*, p. 102.

31. Ibid., pp. 98–99.

32. Ibid., p. 26–29. Segmentary communities may avoid central/ authoritarian tyranny, Gellner argues, but in their failure to shake off the

tyranny of ritual and kinship they cannot qualify as civil societies.

33. See my review of *Conditions of Liberty* in *Canadian Journal of Law and Society*, 11(1996), p. 307.

34. See D. Eickelman, 'Inside the Islamic Reformation,' *Wilson Quarterly*, 22 (1998), p. 80; J.L. Esposito and J.O. Voll, *Islam and Democracy* (New York and Oxford, 1996); E. Ozdalga, 'Civil Society and Its Enemies,' in Elizabeth Ozdalga and Sune Persson, ed., *Civil Society, Democracy and the Muslim World* (Istanbul, 2000) p. 73.

35. J. Habermas, *Moral Consciousness and Communicative Action*, trans. C. Lenhardt and S.W. Nicholson (Cambridge, 1992), discussed in my remarks in the introduction to this volume.

36. Quoted in D.H. Cole, 'An Unqualified Human Good: E.P. Thompson and the Rule of Law,' *Journal of Law and Society*, 28:2 (2001), pp. 177–203, at p. 182. Cole shows that Thompson's 'minimal conception' of the rule of law – a functional view that contrasts with more elaborate, ideology-ridden definitions – allowed him to be derisive about the workings of the law and yet laud it as an institution.

37. T. Carothers, 'The Rule of Law Revival,' *Foreign Affairs*, 77 (1998), pp. 95–106, at p. 96.

38. See, for example, Karen Armstrong, *The Battle for God* (London, 2000); C.G.A. Bryant, 'Civic Nation, Civil Society, Civil Religion,' in *Civil Society: Theory, History, Comparison*, pp. 136–57; R. Coles, *The Secular Mind* (Princeton, NJ, 1999); and citations at notes 1 and 22 above.

39. Gellner, *Conditions of Liberty*, at p. 5.

40. While this conceptual opposition was accentuated by the ideological clashes of the Cold War, so that Soviet bloc states favoured socio-economic rights as against the civil-political rights espoused by Western states, the roots of the conflict can be traced within the liberal tradition itself. Taylor has shown this persuasively in outlining the competing 'Lockean' and 'civic humanist' approaches to civil society: 'Cross-Purposes: The Liberal-Communitarian Debate,' pp. 197–203.

41. John Keane, *Civil Society: Old Images, New Visions* (Cambridge, UK, 1998), p. 80.

42. Ibid., pp. 52–57, 79–89. Keane tends to use 'virtue' and 'value' somewhat loosely and interchangeably here.

43. Ibid., p. 56.

44. See, *inter alia*, A. An-Na'im, 'The Synergy and Interdependence of Human Rights, Religion and Secularism,' *Polylog*, 2 (2001), pp. 1–43 (*www.polylog.org/them/2.1/fcs7-en.htm*), and his 'Human Rights in the Mus-

lim World: Socio-Political Conditions and Scriptural Imperatives,' *Harvard Human Rights Journal*, 3 (1990), p. 13; M. Arkoun, 'The Ideal Community,' 'The Person,' and 'Ethics and Politics,' in *Rethinking Islam*, trans. R.D. Lee (Boulder, CO and Oxford, 1994); S.J. Al-Azm, 'Is Islam Secularizable?' in *Civil Society, Democracy and the Muslim World*, pp. 17–22; A. Filali-Ansari, 'Can Modern Rationality Shape a New Religiosity? Mohamed Abdel Jabri and the Paradox of Islam and Modernity,' in J. Cooper et al., ed., *Islam and Modernity* (London and New York, 2000), pp. 156–71; N. Madjid, 'Potential Islamic Doctrinal Resources for the Establishment and Appreciation of the Modern Concept of Civil Society,' in N. Mitsuo et al., ed., *Islam and Civil Society in Southeast Asia* (Singapore, 2001), pp. 149–63; C. Muzaffar, 'Ethnicity, Ethnic Conflict and Human Rights in Malaysia,' in C.E. Welch and V.A. Leary, ed., *Asian Perspectives on Human Rights* (Boulder, CO, 1990), pp. 107–41; F. Rahman, 'Law and Ethics in Islam,' in *Ethics in Islam*, pp. 3–15; Sadri and Sadri, ed., *Reason, Freedom and Democracy in Islam: Essential Writings of 'Abdolkarim Soroush*, Chapters 3 and 7; R. Wright, 'Two Visions of Reformation' (on Soroush and Ghannouchi), *Journal of Democracy*, 7 (1996), pp. 64–75; Tibi, *Islam between Culture and Politics*.

45. B. Lewis, *The Multiple Identities of the Middle East* (New York, 2001), pp.28–29.

46. Arkoun, 'Ethics and Politics,' at p. 117.

47. Walzer, *al-Farabi on the Perfect State*, pp. 229–59.

48. See Marshall Hodgson, *The Venture of Islam: Conscience and History in a World Civilization* (Chicago and London, 1974), vol. 1, pp. 444–95.

49. Miskawayh, *The Refinement of Character*, trans. C.K. Zurayk (Beirut, 1968).

50. Al-Tusi, *The Nasirean Ethics*.

51. See Fakhry, *Ethical Theories in Islam*, pp. 61–99.

52. Ibid., pp. 78–92.

53. Ibid., pp. 193–206; Arkoun, *Rethinking Islam*, p. 118. See generally, M.A. Quasem, *The Ethics of al-Ghazali: a Composite Ethics in Islam* (Petaling Jaya, Malaysia, 1976).

54. Rahman, 'Ethics in Islam,' especially at p. 4.

55. See Muhammad Iqbal, *The Reconstruction of Religious Thought in Islam* (Lahore, 1962), especially at p. 178. While *ijtihad* was more curtailed in the Sunni than Shi'i tradition, where imams and ayatollahs continued to exercise it, the innovative impulses of the early years were certainly attenuated even in the latter. See generally B. Weiss, 'Interpretation in Islamic Law: The Process of Ijtihad,' *American Journal of Comparative Law*, 26 (1978),

p. 199.

56. There were exceptions, such as Iran's Shi'i *'ulama* who held out against pre-Revolutionary despotisms through much of the 20th century, and likewise al-Azhar's Sunni *'ulama* in Cairo. But such resistance became, by and large, symbols less of ethical authority and autonomy than of rigid traditionalism in the face of 'secular modernity'.

57. In which al-Ghazali himself, for all his theological stature, performed an important part amid the Turko-Arabian tensions of the Saljuq period in the late 11th century: see G. Makdisi, 'The Marriage of Tughril Beg', *International Journal of Middle East Studies* (1970), pp. 259–75.

58. F. Kazemi, 'Civil Society and Iranian Politics', in A.R. Norton, ed., *Civil Society in the Middle East* (Leiden and New York, 1996), vol. 2, p. 119, at pp. 123–26; A. Banuazizi, 'Faltering Legitimacy: The Ruling Clerics and Civil Society in Contemporary Iran', *International Journal of Politics, Culture and Society*, 8 (1995), p. 563; R. Wright, *The Last Great Revolution: Turmoil and Transformation in Iran* (New York, 2000), pp. 32–76, 243–88. The validity of the *Velayat-e-Faqih* notion in Shi'i theology and praxis is disputed; for many, it is simply an ideological tool to preserve clerical political dominance. See Soroush, *Reason, Freedom and Democracy in Islam*, pp. 63–64.

59. See M. Fandy, *Saudi Arabia and the Politics of Dissent* (New York, 2001); J. Teitelbaum, *Holier than Thou: Saudi Arabia's Islamic Opposition* (Washington DC, 2000).

60. See A.S. Moussali, 'Modern Islamic Fundamentalist Discourses on Civil Society, Pluralism and Democracy', in *Civil Society in the Middle East*, vol. 1, p. 79; T. McDaniel, 'The Strange Career of Radical Islam', in J.N. Wasserstrom et al., ed., *Human Rights and Revolutions* (Oxford and New York, 2000), pp. 211–29; Human Rights Watch, *World Report 2002* (New York and London, 2002); Z. Hussain, '"Blasphemy" doctor is sentenced to death', *The Times* (London), (21 August 2001), p. 11 (on a verdict against a medical professor, Younus Shaikh, under Pakistan's blasphemy law).

61. Ibn al-Jawzi, *Talbis Iblis* (Cairo, 1928); A. Abdal-Raziq, *al-Islam wa usul al-hukm* (Cairo, 1925). See the discussion on this issue in Tibi, *Islam between Culture and Politics*, pp. 128, 163–64.

62. See Ilkay Sunar, 'Civil Society and Islam', in *Civil Society, Democracy and the Muslim World*, pp. 9–15; L. Carl Brown, *Religion and State: The Muslim Approach to Politics* (New York, 2000), notably at pp. 31–42.

63. Soroush in *Reason, Freedom, and Democracy in Islam*, pp. 39–53.

64. Ibid., at pp. 105–21, quote at p. 120.

65. M. Boroujerdi, 'The Paradoxes of Politics in Postrevolutionary Iran', in

J.L. Esposito and R.K. Ramazani, ed., *Iran at the Crossroads* (New York, 2001), pp. 13–27, at p. 24. See also M. Kamrava, 'The Civil Society Discourse in Iran,' *British Journal of Middle Eastern Studies*, 28 (2001), pp. 165–85, remarking on today's 'more measured and less ebullient' quality of a reborn intellectual life (at p. 184).

66. T. Faradov, 'Religiosity and Civic Culture in Post-Soviet Azerbaijan: A Sociological Perspective,' in Sajoo, ed., *Civil Society in the Muslim World: Contemporary Perspectives*, pp. 194–213.

67. Although 63.4 per cent of respondents identified themselves as 'believers,' 57.6 per cent said they did not observe any of the basic religious obligations, and 82.3 per cent said they did not pray formally.

68. A. Carkoglu, 'Religion and Public Policy in Turkey,' *Institute for the Study of Islam in the Modern World (ISIM) Newsletter*, 8 (2001), p. 29 (report on the 'Political Islam in Turkey' project).

69. See, for instance, M.M. Howard, 'The Weakness of Postcommunist Civil Society,' *Journal of Democracy*, 13 (2002), pp. 157–69.

70. D. Kandiyoti, 'Rural Livelihoods and Social Networks in Uzbekistan,' *Central Asian Survey*, 17 (1998), pp. 561–78; Oliver Roy, 'Kolkhoz and Civil Society in the Independent States of Central Asia,' in M.H. Ruffin and D. Waugh, ed., *Civil Society in Central Asia* (Seattle and London, 1999), p. 109.

71. E. Kalaycioglu, 'Civil Society in Turkey: Continuity and Change?' in B.W. Beeley, ed., *Turkish Transformation – New Century, New Challenges* (Walkington, 2002); N. Gole, 'Authoritarian Secularism and Islamist Politics: The Case of Turkey,' in *Civil Society in the Middle East*, vol. 2, p. 17.

72. Fiduciary obligations on the part of private and public custodians of wealth are a well-known facet of Islamic tradition, as is the *shura* principle of decision-making by consultation with those who will be affected.

73. See Z. Mir-Hosseini, *Islam and Gender: The Religious Debate in Contemporary Iran* (London, 2000), especially pp. 103–4, 128–43, 241–46 (conversation with Abdolkarim Soroush, on the limits of the law). See also Wright, *The Last Great Revolution*, pp. 133–87.

74. Paul Ricoeur, *Main Trends in Philosophy* (New York, 1979), p. 226: 'A violence that speaks ... is exposing itself to the gravitational pull of Reason and already beginning to renege on its own character as violence.'

75. R.B. Pippin, 'The Ethical Status of Civility?,' in L.S. Rouner, ed., *Civility* (Notre Dame, IN, 2000), pp. 103–17, at p. 106.

76. See Halliday, *Two Hours that Shook the World*, pp. 51–68, 193–211; Armstrong, *The Battle for God*, Part 2 ('Fundamentalism').

77. International legal norms pointedly disallow the violation of fundamental rights in the name of advancing those rights. The premier rights activist group, Amnesty International, does not campaign on behalf of individuals as 'prisoners of conscience' if they have used violence to further their ends. At the same time, pleas by Amnesty and Human Rights Watch against civic subversion by state-violence in the 'war on terror' have yet to be heeded. It should also be recognized that the large-scale mobilization of political violence by 'radical Islamists' is hardly the growing trend that it is often portrayed to be today, as Gilles Keppel persuasively shows in *Jihad: The Trail of Political Islam* (London and Cambridge, MA, 2002).

78. Typically, a widely-quoted tradition has Muhammad saying to his companions on returning from battle that they were now headed for 'the greater jihad', of expunging wrongdoing from one's self and community.

79. In this context, the late, much-revered activist and scholar, Mahmoud Mohamed Taha, postulated a distinction between the Qur'an's Meccan verses with their universalist articulation of ideals, and the subsequent Medinan verses that reflected the hard realities of resistance to the Prophet's mission. For Taha, and his best-known disciple, Abduallahi An-Na'im, nonviolence is to be grounded in the universalism of the Meccan Revelation. For a succinct exposition, see D.L. Smith-Christopher, "'That was Then...": Debating Nonviolence within the Textual Traditions of Judaism, Christianity, and Islam,' in J. Runzo and N.M. Martin, ed., *Ethics in the World Religions* (New York and Oxford, 2001), pp. 256–59.

80. D.M. Donaldson, *Studies in Muslim Ethics* (London, 1953), p. 70.

81. Qur'an, 65:1, 16:33. See Hourani, *Reason and Tradition in Islamic Ethics.*

82. T. Izutsu, *God and Man in the Koran: Semantics of the Koranic Weltanschauung* (Tokyo, 1964), p. 216. On the shared views of Ignatius Goldziher and Charles Pellat, see F. Denny, 'Ethics and the Qur'an: Community and World View,' in Hovannisian, ed., *Ethics in Islam*, pp. 114–5.

83. R. Falk, *Religion and Humane Governance* (New York and Basingstoke, UK, 2001), pp. 143–56. In the Iranian instance, Falk observes that initial restraint on the part of the *'ulama* opposing the Shah was tactical, and soon gave way to the systematic use of political violence in maintaining the new regime. However, he does not consider the possibility that the initial opposition was in fact principled on the part of a different set of leaders from those who eventually came to control the regime.

84. Ibid., at p. 3.

85. V. Jabri, *Discourses on Violence: Conflict Analysis Reconsidered* (New

York, 1996), p. 120, building on Benedict Anderson's much-quoted *Imagined Communities: Reflections on the Origin and Spread of Nationalism* (London, 1991). See also the novelist Amin Maalouf's elegant essay, *In the Name of Identity: Violence and the Need to Belong*, trans. B. Bray (New York, 2000), especially pp. 96–97, 100.

86. I. Serageldin, 'Mirrors and Windows: Redefining the Boundaries of the Mind,' *American Journal of Islamic Social Sciences*, 11 (1994), pp. 79–107, at pp. 88–89. Serageldin argues that society's felt need to preserve cohesion, especially in times of rapid change, strengthens the influence of traditional elements on the collective ethos, at the expense of deeper commitments that might otherwise filter and shape those elements.

87. See Taylor, *The Ethics of Authenticity*, especially pp. 4–11, and Saul, *On Equilibrium*, pp. 297–308 (drawing on Taylor).

88. Visser, *Beyond Fate: The 2002 Massey Lectures*, pp. 106–7.

89. Tibi, *Islam between Culture and Politics*, especially at pp. 69–81.

Chapter 3: A Humanist Ethos: The Dance of Secular and Religious

1. For a trenchant reflection on the currents of religious ethics that underlie some of the key claims in Rawls' theories of justice (notably in his *Lectures on the History of Moral Philosophy* (Cambridge, MA, 2000), however, see Paul Berkowitz, 'John Rawls and the Liberal Faith,' *The Wilson Quarterly*, 26:2 (2002), pp. 60–69.

2. E. Durkheim, *De la division du travail social* (4th ed. Paris, 1922), pp. 143–44.

3. For a succinct account that links French, European and global trends in this regard, see Nikki Keddie, 'Secularism and its Discontents,' *Daedalus*, 132:3 (2003), pp. 14–30. More generally see Asad, *Formations of the Secular* and Chadwick, *The Secularization of the European Mind in the Nineteenth Century*.

4. 283 U.S. 605 (1931).

5. Ibid., at p. 622.

6. See Charles Reid, 'The Religious Conscience,' in H. Heclo and W.M. McClay, ed., *Religion Returns to the Public Square: Faith and Policy in America* (Washington DC, 2003), pp. 63–110.

7. For an acclaimed account see David Remnick, *King of the World: Muhammad Ali and the Rise of an American Hero* (New York, 1998).

8. Pew Research Center for the People and the Press, Global Attitudes Project, *Among Wealthy Nations - U.S. Stands Alone in Its Embrace of Religion*

(Washington DC, 2002): *http://people-press.org/reports/pdf/167.pdf.*

9. Taylor, *Varieties of Religion Today: William James Revisited*, pp. 93–107.

10. See Seligman, *The Idea of Civil Society.*

11. Huntington, *The Clash of Civilizations and the Remaking of World Order.* See also Pye, *Asian Power and Politics: The Cultural Dimensions of Authority*; and Francis Fukuyama, *The End of History and the Last Man* (New York and Toronto, 1992).

12. See Sajoo, 'Muslims beware,' *The Guardian*, p. 22; Edward Said, 'Islam and the West are inadequate banners,' *The Observer* (16 September 2001): *http://www.observer.co.uk/comment/story/0,6903,552764,00.html.*

13. 'Dead and Missing,' *The New York Times* (4 April 2002), p. A11.

14. Huntington, *The Clash of Civilizations*, p. 258, adding that only Chinese civilizations matches Islam in this regard, and that Islam 'glorifies military virtues' (p. 263).

15. Ibid., p. 307.

16. B. Lewis, *What Went Wrong: Western Impact and Middle Eastern Response* (New York, 2002).

17. For a trenchant challenge to the book's historical method and veracity, see Juan Cole review, *Global Dialogue*, 4:4 (2002); *www.juancole.com/essays/revlew.htm.*

18. Sponsored by the Donner Canadian Foundation and broadcast on CBC Radio One's 'Ideas' series on 24 October, 2002.

19. *The New Yorker* (19 November 2001), pp. 50–63.

20. CBC Radio One's 'Ideas' broadcast, 23 October, 2002.

21. Lewis, 'Islam in Revolt,' pp. 57–63.

22. W. McClay, 'Two Concepts of Secularism,' in Heclo and McClay, ed., *Religion Returns to the Public Square: Faith and Policy in America*, pp. 31–61, at 53, citing Lewis's *What Went Wrong.*

23. 'The Revolt of Islam,' pp. 60, 50. For a more sophisticated analysis – supported by empirical evidence – that suggests a different picture, see Jason Burke, *Al-Qaeda: Casting a Shadow of Terror* (London, 2003).

24. Huntington, *The Clash of Civilizations*, p. 217.

25. Ibid., p. 263.

26. Lenn Goodman, 'Humanism and Islamic Ethics,' *Logos*, 1:2 (2002): *http://logosonline.home.igc.org/goodman.htm*; extracted from his *Islamic Humanism: Experiments in Classical Islam* (Oxford, forthcoming).

27. B. Lewis, 'The Roots of Muslim Rage,' (September 1990), p. 49.

28. See John Kelsay, *Islam and War: A Study in Comparative Ethics* (Lou-

isville, KY, 1993), pp. 46–47.

29. See, *inter alia*, S. Hashmi, 'Interpreting the Islamic Ethics of War and Peace,' in Hashmi, ed., *Islamic Political Ethics: Civil Society, Pluralism, and Conflict*, pp. 194–216;. J.T. Johnson and J. Kelsay, ed., *Cross, Crescent and Sword: The Justification and Limitation of War in Western and Islamic Tradition* (Westport, CT, 1990); Kelsay, *Islam and War, supra*. pp. 44–55. It is interesting that Christian ethics were invoked by Nobel laureate and former U.S President Jimmy Carter in his opposition to the war on Iraq: 'Just War – Or A Just War ?' *The New York Times*, 9 March 2003: *www.nytimes.com/2003/03/09/opinion/09CART.html*.

30. René Girard, *The Scapegoat*, trans. Y. Freccero, originally published as *Le Bouc emissaire* (Paris, 1982), and *I See Satan Fall Like Lightening*, trans. J.G. Williams (Maryknoll, NY, 2001), originally *Je vois Satan tomber comme l'éclair* (Paris, 1999); Leo D. Lefebure, *Revelation, the Religions, and Violence* (Maryknoll, NY, 2000); Charles Taylor, 'Sacred Killing: The Roots of Violence,' pp. 11–16, and Mary Malone, 'Cosmic Showdown: The Road to Violence in the Christian Tradition,' pp. 27–30, in *Voices Across Boundaries*, 1:1 (2003).

31. August C. Krey, *The First Crusade: The Accounts of Eyewitnesses and Participants* (Princeton and London, 1921), p. 260; cited in Karen Armstrong, *Jerusalem: One City, Three Faiths* (New York, 1996), p. 274.

32. Armstrong, *Jerusalem: One City, Three Faiths*, pp. 293–94 (quote at p. 294).

33. Ibid., p. 299.

34. 'Shamir on Terrorism (1943),' *Middle East Report* (May-June 1988), p. 55. Shamir was then leader of the Irgun, a Jewish terrorist gang primarily fighting colonial Britain.

35. Hourani, *Reason and Tradition in Islamic Ethics*, p. 86. See also Carl Ernst, *Following Muhammad: Rethinking Islam in the Contemporary World* (Chapel Hill, NC, 2003), arguing that the rationality of Muslim ethics induced a reasoned reading of scriptural norms that – contrary to Lenn Goodman's claim – rarely became authoritarian (pp. 109–10).

36. The quoted phrase is Fazlur Rahman's: see S. Nomanul Haq, 'Islam and Ecology: Toward Retrieval and Reconstruction,' *Daedalus* (American Academy of Arts and Sciences), 130:4 (2001), pp. 141–78; at p. 151: *http://www.daedalus.amacad.org/issues/fall2001/haq.htm*.

37. Quoted ibid., at p. 155, from the Ikhwan al-Safa, *Dispute Between Man and Animals*, trans. J. Platt (London, 1869). It is in this spirit that Nasir-i Khusraw (1004–1077) ponders in his *Diwan*, 'Why is the crane, lamenting without meaning, not so contemptible while we are fools?' To which he later

answers: 'The Word was given us among all animals – we are the only ones among whom a prophet arose!' Quoted in Annemarie Schimmel, *Make a Shield from Wisdom: Selected Verses from Nasir-i Khusraw's Diwan* (London, 2001), p. 33.

38. See Majid Fakhry, 'Philosophy and Theology: From the Eighth Century C.E. to the Present,' in Esposito, ed., *The Oxford History of Islam*, pp. 260–303, at 277–81.

39. Ibid., pp.285–86.

40. M.K. Masud, 'The Scope of Pluralism in Islamic Moral Traditions,' in *Islamic Political Ethics, supra*, pp. 135–47, at 137.

41. Ahmed Dallal, 'Science, Medicine and Technology: The Making of a Scientific Culture,' in *The Oxford History of Islam, supra*, pp. 155–213, at pp. 205–7.

42. See Jonathan Bloom, *Paper Before Print: The History and Impact of Paper in the Islamic World* (New Haven, CT and London, 2001), pp. 203–13.

43. Ibid., 125–59, especially at pp. 136–37.

44. Ibid., pp. 116–23.

45. Ibid., p. 122.

46. Fakhry, 'Philosophy and Theology,' pp. 280–84.

47. Bernard Lewis, *The Jews of Islam* (Princeton, NJ, 1987), pp. 3–4.

48. Maria Rosa Menoca, *The Ornament of the World: How Muslims, Jews and Christians Created a Culture of Tolerance in Medieval Spain* (New York and London, 2002); quote at p. 12.

49. Fakhry, 'Philosophy and Theology,' pp. 291–93.

50. See, *inter alia*, Keddie, 'Secularism and its Discontents,' *supra*; Azzam Tamimi and J.L. Esposito, ed., *Islam and Secularism in the Middle East* (London, 2000); M.K. Masud, *Muslim Jurists' Quest for the Normative Basis of Shari'a* (Leiden, 2001); Ebrahim Moosa, 'Configuring Muslim Thought,' *ISIM* (International Institute for the Study of Islam in the Modern World, Leiden), *Newsletter*, 12 (2003), pp. 30–31.

51. Reza Davari-Ardakani, *Falsafih dar Buhran* [Philosophy in Crisis] (Tehran, 1994), p. 65. Davari contends that the Enlightenment's individualist reason or *nafsiyyat* has subverted Muslim public culture with 'Westoxication', a trend that he also considers to have undermined the West's own fidelity to a superior pre-humanist ethos. For a succinct synopsis of Davari's thought, see Farzin Vahdat, 'Post-Revolutionary Islamic Discourses on Modernity in Iran: Expansion and Contraction of Human Subjectivity,' *International Journal of Middle East Studies* (November, 2003), pp. 559–631, notably at pp. 603–12.

52. Fazlur Rahman, *Islam and Modernity: Transformation of an Intellectual*

Tradition (Chicago and London, 1982), pp. 154–57; 'Law and Ethics in Islam,' *supra*, at p. 4.

53. *Taqwa* is invoked, in one account, over 200 times in the Qur'an in one form or another: Azim Nanji, 'The Ethical Tradition in Islam,' in A. Nanji, ed., *The Muslim Almanac* (New York, 1996), pp. 205–11, at p. 206. For Majid Fakhry, the term *al-birr*, translated as 'righteousness', best captures the 'moral and religious spirit' of the Qur'an; he translates *taqwa* as 'piety', which in any case is also a cognate of *al-birr*: Fakhry, *Ethical Theories in Islam*, pp. 12–13.

54. Rahman, *Islam and Modernity*, *supra*, pp. 154–55; Masud, 'The Scope of Pluralism in Islamic Moral Traditions,' *supra*, p. 139–40.

55. See generally, Mohammad Hashim Kamali, 'Law and Society: The Interplay of Revelation and Reason in the Shari'a,' in *The Oxford History of Islam*, *supra*, pp. 107–53.

56. Masud, 'The Scope of Pluralism in Islamic Moral Traditions,' pp. 141–45, and in the same volume, Dale Eickelman, 'Islam and Ethical Pluralism,' pp. 115–34. See also Vincent Connell, 'From Shariah to Taqwa: Islam and Ethics,' in his chapter 'Fruit of the Tree of Knowledge,' in *The Oxford History of Islam*, *supra*, pp. 95–105.

57. A.E. Mayer, *Islam and Human Rights: Tradition and Politics* (Boulder, CO, 1999), p. 192.

58. M. Shahrur, *The Book and the Qur'an: A Contemporary Interpretation* (Damascus, 1990). See Dale Eickelman, 'Islamic Liberalism Strikes Back,' *Middle East Studies Association Bulletin*, 27:2 (1993), pp. 163–68.

59. See Afshin Molavi, 'The Disenchantment,' *Wilson Quarterly* (Winter 2003), pp. 48–55, at pp. 51–52.

60. A. Soroush, 'Reforming the Revolution,' *Index on Censorship* (London), (January 2002), pp. 64–77, at p. 77. In this vein, see Azar Nafisi's appreciation of the potency of literature-as-liberation in her *Reading Lolita in Tehran: A Memoir in Books*.

61. See Tapper, *The New Iranian Cinema: Politics, Representation and Identity*; Dabashi, *Close Up: Iranian Cinema*.

62. D. Eickelman, 'Islam and Ethical Pluralism,' pp. 123–27.

63. Ersin Kalaycioglu, 'State and Civil Society in Turkey: Democracy, Development and Protest,' in Sajoo, ed. *Civil Society in the Muslim World: Contemporary Perspectives*, pp. 247–72, at pp. 262–68.

64. See S. Nanes, 'Fighting Honor Crimes: Evidence of Civil Society in Jordan,' *The Middle East Journal*, 57:1 (2003), pp. 112–29, at p. 125.

65. Ibid., p. 122.

66. S. Akiner, 'Prospects for Civil Society in Tajikistan,' in Sajoo, ed., *Civil*

Society in the Muslim World, supra, pp. 149–193, at pp. 182–86.

67. Ibid., pp. 177–82, at p. 181.

68. Dale Eickelman and Jon Anderson, ed., *New Media in the Muslim World: The Emerging Public Sphere* (2nd ed., Bloomington and Indianapolis, IN, 2003).

69. Aziz Al-Azmeh, *Islams and Modernities* (2nd ed., New York, 1996).

70. See, *inter alia,* Yvonne Haddad, ed., *Muslims in the West: From Sojourners to Citizens* (New York, 2002); John L. Esposito and Francois Burgat, ed., *Modernizing Islam: Religion in the Public Sphere in Europe and the Middle East* (London, 2003).

71. Gary Bunt, *Virtually Islamic* (Cardiff, 2000), p. 17.

72. See, for example, Ebrahimian, Laleh D., 'Socio-economic Development in Iran Through Information and Communications Technology,' *The Middle East Journal,* 57:1 (2003), pp. 93–111, on the disparity in 'connectivity' between the U.S. and Iran.

73. See their 'Redefining Muslim Publics,' pp. 1–18, as well as J. Anderson, 'The Internet and Islam's New Interpreters,' pp. 41–56, and Augustus R. Norton, 'The New Media, Civic Pluralism, and the Slowly Retreating State,' pp. 19–28, in Eickelman and Anderson, ed., *New Media in the Muslim World: The Emerging Public Sphere, supra.* See more generally, Leslie David Simon et al., *Democracy and the Internet: Allies or Adversaries?* (Washington DC, 2003).

74. See, for example, Justin Webb, 'America's deep Christian faith,' BBC World News (14 March 2003): *http://news.bbc.co.uk/go/pr/fr//2/hi/ programmes/from_our_own_correspondent/2850485.stm*; Ahmed, *Islam Under Siege: Living Dangerously in a Post-Honour World,* pp. 25–39.

75. J. Casanova, 'What is a Public Religion?' in *Religion Returns to the Public Square: Faith and Policy in America, supra,* pp. 111–39, at p. 135, 139.

76. Ibid., p. 134.

77. Ibid.

78. See Haddad, ed., *Muslims in the West: From Sojourners to Citizens, supra*; Sadik Harchoui, 'Church and State in Multicultural Society,' *ISIM Newsletter* (Institute for the Study of Islam in the Modern World, Leiden, Netherlands), 11 (2002), p. 12: *http://www.isim.nl.*

79. See especially Abdullahi An-Na'im, 'The Synergy and Interdependence of Human Rights, Religion and Secularism,' *Polylog* (Online), 2:1 (2001): *http://www.polylog.org/them/2.1/fcs7-en.htm*; and his *Toward an Islamic Reformation: Civil Liberties, Human Rights and International Law* (Syracuse, NJ,

1990).

80. Dworkin, *Sovereign Virtue: The Theory and Practice of Equality*, pp. 212–13.

81. See Michael Ignatieff, *Blood and Belonging: Journeys into the New Nationalism* (London and Toronto, 1993).

82. 'The Civilization of Difference', 2003 LaFontaine-Baldwin lecture, Halifax, Nova Scotia (7 March 2003): *http://www.lafontaine-baldwin.com*.

Chapter 4: Pluralist Governance

1. Rahman, *Islam and Modernity: Transformation of an Intellectual Tradition*, pp. 23–24.

2. See United Nations Development Program (UNDP), 'Liberating human capabilities: governance, human development and the Arab world', *Arab Human Development Report 2002* (New York, 2002), pp. 105–20.

3. Ibid., p. 107, drawing upon the *Nahj al-Balagha* of Imam 'Ali, as interpreted by the Egyptian jurist and social activist, Mohammad Abdou: Part 1 (2nd ed., Beirut, 1985).

4. 'The new men, and women, in charge', *The Economist* (London), (17 July 2003); *http://www.economist.com/displaystory.cfm?story_id=1924409*. Part of the rationale for the styling was that an 'advisory' body, as it was formerly called, would command far less legitimacy than a 'governing' one, especially since the principal occupying power, the United States, appointed its 25 members.

5. Hasan bin Talal, 'Seeing Iraq's Future by Looking at its Past' (op-ed), *The New York Times* (18 July 2003); *http://www.nytimes.com/2003/07/18/opinion/18TALA.html*. On the context of 'democratic reconstruction' in which the Council operates, where ideological and physical coercion by U.S. administrators appears to be the dominant mode of decision-making, see the analysis by Robert Fisk, 'US fostering sinister sort of democracy', *The Independent* (London), (1 August 2003); syndicated at *http://www.nzherald.co.nz/storyprint.cfm?storyID=3515705*. Again, the habitual arbitrary confiscation of private property by the occupying forces bodes ill for fostering the rule of law: Shaila Dewan, 'Iraqis struggle to retrieve goods from G.I.s', *The New York Times* (3 August 2003); *http://www.nytimes.com/2003/08/03/international/worldspecial/03THEF.html*. On the wider issue of governance that comes to grips with Islamic civic principles, see especially Noah Feldman, *After Jihad: America and the Struggle for Islamic Democracy* (New York, 2003).

6. Larry Goodson, 'Afghanistan's Long Road to Reconstruction,' *Journal of Democracy*, 14:1 (2003), pp. 82–99, at p. 89. Goodson was an advisor to the Loya Jirga, the postwar assembly that established the formal transitional government led by President Hamid Karzai, and is the author of *Afghanistan's Endless War: State Failure, Regional Politics, and the Rise of the Taliban* (Washington, DC, 2000). See also Reza Aslan, 'Why Religion Must Play a Role in Iran,' *The New York Times* (18 July 2003); *http://www.nytimes.com/2003/07/18/opinion/18ASLA.html* (arguing that the 'religious democracy' called for by student protesters is not tantamount to theocracy, and better reflects the tenor of public preference than Western-style democracy).

7. See Gellner, *Conditions of Liberty: Civil Society and its Rivals*, especially at pp. 61–80.

8. Edward Shils, 'The Virtue of Civil Society,' in *Government and Opposition*, lecture delivered at the Athenaeum Club (22 January 1991), at pp. 11–12; reprinted in Hodgkinson and Foley, ed., *The Civil Society Reader*, pp. 292–305, at p. 299.

9. See Seligman, *The Idea of Civil Society*, pp. 15–58.

10. Selma van Londen and Arie de Ruijter make the case for compatibility over commonality in the context of managing the balance of global and local forces that produce plural identities: 'Managing Diversity in a Globalizing World,' Workshop Paper sponsored by the Fondazione Eni Enrico Mattei (January 2003): *http://www.feem.it/web/activ/_wp.html*. They argue that aiming at shared values (commonality) requires assimilation that denies diversity, while avoiding forced pursuits of the common good (compatibility) allows maximum space for difference. However, the pragmatism of this approach fails to justify it is as anything more than a 'conflict avoidance' model of tolerance, well short of the aspirations of a pluralist model that builds on shared citizenship and community.

11. See B.E. Vaughn and K. Mlekov, 'A Stage Model of Developing an Inclusive Community,' Workshop paper sponsored by the Fondazione Eni Enrico Mattei (January 2003): *http://www.feem.it/web/activ/_wp.html*. The authors call the 'achieved definition' a 'Third Culture' that is a hybrid of host and migrant cultures, based primarily on empirical observation in California and Stockholm, Sweden. The logic of hybridized identity as a pluralist outcome, however, clearly applies well beyond such contextual confines.

12. *Democracy in America*, trans. Henry Reeve, with a critical appraisal by John Stuart Mill (New York, 1961). While Tocqueville alludes to the distinctive realities of the civic lives of these groups – notably in vol. 2, section 3 – he draws no significant inferences about the implications for democracy.

13. In *Plessey v. Ferguson* (1896), 163 U.S. 537.

14. In Brown v. Board of Education (1954), 347 U.S. 483.

15. *Hadith* compilations of Bukhari (no. 1312), Muslim (no. 2222) and Nasa'i (no. 1920).

16. See especially Lawrence Rosen, *The Culture of Islam: Changing Aspects of Contemporary Muslim Life* (Chicago and London, 2002), pp. 58–65.

17. See Brown, *Religion and State: The Muslim Approach to Politics*, especially at pp. 60–75.

18. A. Picard and C. Alphonso, 'Canadians ratchet up criticism of travel advisory,' *The Globe and Mail*, (25 April 2003), p. A1; Jennifer Lewington, 'Blitz aims to calm fears of SARS, get tourists back,' *The Globe and Mail* (25 April 2003), p. A7. See generally on SARS the World Health Organization (WHO)'s extensive briefings at *http://www.who.int/csr/sars/en/index.html.*

19. See Sheema Khan, 'Canadians still nasty to Muslims' (op-ed feature), *The Globe and Mail* (1 May 2003), p. A19.

20. Clifford Krauss, 'A Sikh boy's little dagger sets off a mighty din,' *The New York Times* (5 June 2002), p. A4; 'The kirpan compromise Quebec won't accept,' (Editorial), *The Globe and Mail* (1 June 2002), p. A18.

21. Miro Cernetig, 'Of free speech, jihad and Harvard racism,' *The Globe and Mail* (1 June 2002); Nader R. Hasan, 'Jihad and Veritas,' *The New York Times* (5 June 2002).

22. Amyn B. Sajoo, 'Our closed open minds,' *The Globe and Mail* (Op-ed feature), (6 June 2002), p. A19.

23. See Afshin Molavi, 'The Disenchantment,' *The Wilson Quarterly* (Winter 2003), pp. 48–55, at p. 51.

24. Fareed Zakari, *The Future of Freedom: Illiberal Democracy at Home and Abroad* (New York, 2003).

25. Huntington, *The Clash of Civilizations and the Remaking of World Order*, pp. 305–8, at p. 305. 'American multiculturalists reject their country's cultural heritage,' insists Huntington, and that they 'wish to create a country of many civilizations, which is to say a country not belonging to any civilization and lacking a cultural core.' (p. 306) This assumes that there is a unitary heritage to embrace for all Americans in the first instance, and that a complex, multi-civilizational identity is a weakness rather than strength even in an age of cultural globalization.

26. Ibid., p. 307.

27. Notably under Articles 13–14 (minorities), 19–20 (general equality) and 64 (group representation). Tribal and regional linguistic freedom in the media and schools is also affirmed, within the context of Persian as the official

language (Art. 15).

28. For example, minority rights are conditional on refraining from 'engaging in conspiracy or activity against Islam and the Islamic Republic of Iran' (Art. 14), which imposes loyalty requirements over and above those of common citizenship; an 'official religion' (Twelver Shi'ism) is proclaimed (Art. 12) with all that this implies for the identity of its governors; and the rule of law framework within which the judiciary is mandated is explicitly subject to 'ideological conformity' (Preamble). Moreover, the discrepancy between normative and practical respect for minorities in Iran has been widely documented by independent and United Nations human rights agencies.

29. See Amyn B. Sajoo, *Pluralism in 'Old Societies and New States': Emerging ASEAN Contexts* (Singapore, 1994), notably at pp. 31–65.

30. Ahmed, *Islam Under Siege: Living Dangerously in a Post-Honour World*, notably pp. 57–73. More generally, see Michael Ignatieff, *The Warrior's Honor: Ethnic War and the Modern Conscience* (Toronto, 1998), and Chris Hedges, *War is a Force that Gives us Meaning* (New York, 2002).

31. Fourth annual LaFontaine-Baldwin lecture, delivered on 7 March 2003, in Halifax, Nova Scotia, by Beverley McLachlin, Chief Justice of Canada.

32. See generally Abou El Fadl, *The Place of Tolerance in Islam*, and Abdulaziz Sachedina, *The Islamic Roots of Democratic Pluralism* (New York, 2001), especially at pp. 35–36.

33. Havel, *Summer Meditations*, pp. 8, 20, 128.

34. Keynote address by His Highness the Aga Khan (7 September 2002), at the Prince Claus Fund's Conference on Culture and Development, Amsterdam: *http://www.akdn.org/speeches/10_amsterdam.htm*.

35. Ibid.: '[G]overnments, civil societies and the peoples of this world will be unable to build strong pluralist societies with the present level of global cultural ignorance ... Even the most developed countries will need a massive effort to educate the world's youth in a more thoughtful, competent and complete manner ... particularly so in the increasing number of functioning democracies where an informed public plays such a central role ... Developing support for pluralism does not occur naturally in human society. It is a concept which must be nurtured every day, in every forum – in large and small government and private institutions; in civil society organizations working in the arts, culture, and public affairs, in the media; in the law, and in justice – particularly in terms of social justice, such as health, social safety nets and education; and in economic justice, such as employment opportunities and access to financial services.'

36. 'Iran journalists sit in to protest "absence of justice",' *The Globe and Mail* (9 August 2003) *http://globeandmail.com/servlet/story/RTGAM.20030809.wiran0809/BNStory/International/*. The tradition rests on key Qur'anic verses (96:4–5, 68:1) which refer to teaching by the Pen and the integrity of the written word.

37. See, for example, her lyrical *Islam and Democracy: Fear of the Modern World*, trans. M. Lakeland (Cambridge, MA, 2002), which concludes with an invocation of Farid al-Din 'Attar's 12th century poem, *The Conference of the Birds*.

38. Heclo and McClay, ed., *Religion Returns to the Public Square: Faith and Policy in America*.

39. Gellner, *Conditions of Liberty*, pp. 15–29, 50–52.

40. See Niyazi Berkes, *The Development of Secularization in Turkey* (Montreal, 1964), pp. 3–4; Ilkay Sunar, Civil Society and Islam,' pp. 9–15, and Sadiq J. Al-Azm, 'Is Islam Secularizable ?' pp. 17–22, in Ozdalga and Persson, ed., *Civil Society, Democracy and the Muslim World*.

41. See Bunt, *Virtually Islamic*, esp. 13–27; Dale Eickelman and J. Anderson, 'Redefining Muslim Publics,' pp. 1–18, in Eickelman and Anderson, ed., *New Media in the Muslim World: The Emerging Public Sphere*.

42. Pamuk, *My Name is Red*, pp. 160–61.

43. See especially his *The Scapegoat*, and *I See Satan Falling Like Lightning*.

44. There is also the valorization of the lonely but righteous outsider, of whom prime exemplars are Muhammad in the early Meccan phase, the martyrdoms of Imam Husayn at Kerbala in Shi'i tradition, and of Mansur al-Hallaj and al-Suhrawardi in Sufism.

45. Fazlur Rahman, *Major Themes of the Qur'an* (Minneapolis, 1980), pp. 163–64, at 164.

46. Ibid.

47. 'Recognition Without Ethics?' in Marjorie Garber et al., ed., *The Turn to Ethics* (New York and London, 2000), pp. 95–126. The essay is adapted from her Tanner Lecture on Human Values at Stanford University, April 30-May 2, 1996, published as 'Social Justice in the Age of Identity Politics: Redistribution, Recognition and Participation,' in Grethe B. Peterson, ed., *The Tanner Lectures on Human Values* (Salt Lake City, 1998), vol. 19, pp. 1–67.

48. Only in rare cases does Fraser believe that claims for recognition by socio-cultural minorities require ethical judgement, because the matter cannot be disposed of by 'deontological means' (pp. 120–22).

49. Somerville, *The Ethical Canary: Science, Society and the Human Spirit*, pp. 10–12. Talal Asad puts it thus amid the historical interface of civic modernity and tradition in a Muslim context: 'whereas ethics could at one time stand independently of a political organization (although not of collective obligations), in a secular state it presupposes a specific political realm – representative democracy, citizenship, law and order, civil liberties, and so on. For only where there is this public realm can personal ethics become constituted as sovereign and be closely linked to a personally chosen way of life – that is, an aesthetic.' 'Reconfigurations of Law and Ethics in Colonial Egypt,' in his *Formations of the Secular: Christianity, Islam, Modernity*, pp. 254–56, at p. 255.

50. Somerville, pp. 5–9, by which she means the conferral of 'preeminence to the values of personal autonomy and self-determination' against all other claims for social respect, no matter how legitimate. On the other hand, it is often argued that the very individuality of the postmodern Self is only partially captured by rights-talk that levels and universalizes complexity in the name of human equality: see, for example, Costas Douzinas, 'Identity, Recognition, Rights or What Can Hegel Teach Us About Human Rights?' *Journal of Law and Society*, 29 (2002), pp. 379–405.

51. See Elaine Sciolino, 'Chirac backs law to keep signs of faith out of school,' *The New York Times* (18 December 2003); *http://www.nytimes.com/2003/12/18/international/europe/18FRAN.html*; Paul Webster, 'Chirac calls on MPs to ban headscarf,' *The Guardian* (18 December 2003); (*http://www.guardian.co.uk/france/story/0,11882,1109248,00.html*); Cynthia Brown, ed., *Lost Liberties: Ashcroft and the Assault on Personal Freedom* (New York and London, 2003).

52. See T. Govier and W. Verwoerd. 'Taking Wrongs Seriously: A Qualified Defence of Public Apologies,' *Saskatchewan Law Review*, 65 (2002), pp. 139–62. More generally see M. Minow, *Between Vengeance and Forgiveness: Facing History after Genocide and Mass Violence* (Boston, 1998).

53. An instance of such lack of ambition and memory is the claim by William Galston that all one can hope is the exposure to modernity will produce in Muslim societies 'a tolerable degree if not of respect at least of liberty for diverse faiths and ways of life,' in the name of 'political decency': 'Jews, Muslims and the Prospects for Pluralism,' *Daedalus*, 132:3 (2003), pp. 73–77, at p. 77.

Select Bibliography

Abou El Fadl, Khaled. *The Place of Tolerance in Islam*, ed., Joshua Cohen and Ian Lague. Boston, MA, 2002.

Ahmed, Akbar. *Islam Under Siege: Living Dangerously in a Post-Honour World*. Cambridge, 2003.

An-Na'im, Abdullahi. *Toward an Islamic Reformation: Civil Liberties, Human Rights and International Law*. Syracuse, NY, 1990.

——ed., *Human Rights in Cross-Cultural Perspectives: A Quest for Censensus*. Philadelphia, PA, 1992.

——'The Synergy and Interdependence of Human Rights, Religion and Secularism,' *Polylog* (Online), 2:1 (2001): *http://www.polylog.org/them/2.1/fcs7-en.htm*

Archer, John Clark. 'Moslem Ethics,' in E. Hershey Sneath, ed., *The Evolution of Ethics*. New Haven, CT, 1927, pp. 327–56.

Arkoun, Mohammed. 'Ethics and Politics,' in M. Arkoun, *Rethinking Islam*. Boulder, CO, 1996, pp. 114–20.

Asad, Talal. *Formations of the Secular: Christianity, Islam, Modernity*. Stanford, 2003.

Bellah, Robert, et al. *The Good Society*. New York, 1991.

Brockopp, Jonathan, ed. *Islamic Ethics of Life: Abortion, War, and Euthanasia*. Columbia, SC, 2003.

Cahn, S.M. and Peter Markie, ed. *Ethics: History, Theory and Contemporary Issues*. Oxford, 1998.

Clarfield, A.M., M. Gordon, M.H. Markwell and S. Alibhai. 'Ethical Issues in End-of-Life Geriatric Care: The Approach of Three Monotheistic Religions – Judaism, Catholicism, and Islam,' *Journal of the American Geriatric Society*, 51:8 (2003), pp. 1149–54.

Charvet, John. *The Idea of an Ethical Community*. Ithaca, NY, 1995.

Cook, Michael. *Commanding Right and Forbidding Wrong in Islamic Thought*. Cambridge, 2001.

Cornell, Vincent. 'From Shariah to Taqwa,' in John L. Esposito, ed., *The Oxford History of Islam*. Oxford, 1999, pp. 95–105.

Daar, Abdallah S. 'Xenotransplantation and Religion: The Major Monotheistic Religions,' *Xeno*, 2 (1994), pp. 61–64.

—and A. Khitamy. 'Islamic Bioethics' (Bioethics for Clinicians Series), *Canadian Medical Association Journal*, 164:1 (2001); *www.cma.ca/series/ bioethic.com*

Dabashi, Hamid. *Close Up: Iranian Cinema*. London and New York, 2001.

Dalai Lama. *Ethics for the Next Millennium*. New York, 1999.

Dallal, Ahmed. 'Science, Medicine and Technology,' in John L. Esposito, ed., *The Oxford History of Islam*. Oxford, 1999, pp. 155–213.

Deen, Mawil Y.I. 'Islamic Environmental Ethics,' in J.R. Engel and J.G. Engel, *Ethics of Environment and Development: Global Challenge, International Response*. Tucson, AZ, 1990, pp. 189–98.

Donaldson, D.M. *Studies in Muslim Ethics*. London, 1953.

Draz, M.A. *The Moral World of the Qur'an*. London, 2002.

Dworkin, Ronald M. *Sovereign Virtue: The Theory and Practice of Equality*. Cambridge, MA, 2000.

Esmail, Aziz. 'Self, Society, Civility and Islam,' in Amyn B. Sajoo, ed., *Civil Society in the Muslim World*. London, 2002, pp. 61–94.

Fakhry, Majid. *Ethical Theories in Islam*. Leiden, 1991; 2nd ed., 1994.

Feldman, Noah. *After Jihad: America and the Struggle for Islamic Democracy*. New York, 2003.

Fraser, Nancy. 'Recognition without Ethics?' in M. Garber et al., ed., *The Turn to Ethics*. London, 2000, pp. 95–126.

Fukuyama, Francis. *Our Posthuman Future: Consequences of the Biotechnology Revolution*. New York, 2002.

Girard, René. *The Scapegoat*, trans. Y. Freccero. Paris, 1982.

Govier, Trudy and W. Verwoerd. 'Taking Wrongs Seriously: A Qualified Defence of Public Apologies,' *Saskatchewan Law Review*, 65 (2002), pp. 139–62.

Habermas, Jürgen. *The Future of Human Nature*. Cambridge, 2003.

Haq, S. Nomanul. 'Islam and Ecology: Toward Retrieval and Reconstruction,'

Daedalus, 130:4 (2001), pp. 141–78.

Hardy, Paul, ed. *Traditions of Islam: Understanding the Hadith*. London, 2002.

Hashmi, Sohail H., ed. *Islamic Political Ethics: Civil Society, Pluralism and Conflict*. Princeton, 2002.

Heclo, Hugh and W.M. McClay, ed. *Religion Returns to the Public Square: Faith and Policy in America*. Baltimore, MD and London, 2003.

Hong, H.V. and E.H. Hong, ed. and trans., *Kierkegaard's Writings*. Princeton, 1980.

Hourani, George. *Reason and Tradition in Islamic Ethics*. Cambridge, 1985.

Hovannisian, Richard G., ed. *Ethics in Islam*. Malibu, CA, 1985.

Institute of Ismaili Studies, The. *Aga Khan Development Network (AKDN): An Ethical Framework*. London, 2001.

Islamic Organization for Medical Sciences (IOMS). *The Islamic Code of Medical Ethics*. Kuwait, 1981.

Izutsu, Toshiko. *God and Man in the Koran: Semantics of the Koranic Weltanschauung*. Tokyo, 1964.

——*Ethico-Religious Concepts in the Quran*. Montreal, 2002.

Johansen, Baber. *Contingency in a Sacred Law: Legal and Ethical Norms in the Muslim Fiqh*. Leiden, 1999.

Johnson, Mark. *Moral Imagination: Implications of Cognitive Science for Ethics*. Chicago, 1993.

Kamali, M.H. 'Law and Society: The Interplay of Revelation and Reason in the Shariah,' in John L. Esposito, ed., *The Oxford History of Islam*. Oxford, 1999, pp. 107–53.

Keane, John. *Civil Society: Old Images, New Values*. Cambridge, 1998.

Keddie, Nikki. 'Secularization and its Discontents,' *Daedalus*, 132:3 (2003), pp. 14–30.

Kelsay, John. *Islam and War: A Study in Comparative Ethics*. Louiseville, KY, 1993.

Küng, Hans, ed. *Yes to a Global Ethic*. New York, 1996.

Kurzman, Charles, ed. *Liberal Islam: A Sourcebook*. Oxford, 1998.

Lefebure, Leo. *Revelation, Religion, and Violence*. Maryknoll, NY, 2000.

Lerner, Ralph. *Averroes on Plato's Republic*. Ithaca, NY, 1974.

MacIntyre, Alasdair. *After Virtue: A Study in Moral Theory*. Notre Dame, IN, 1984.

Maguire, D.C. *Sacred Choices: The Right to Contraception and Abortion in Ten World Religions*. Minneapolis, MN, 2001.

Masud, M.K. *Shatibi's Philosophy of Islamic Law*. Islamabad, 1995.

Mayer, Ann Elizabeth. *Islam and Human Rights: Tradition and Politics*. 2nd ed., Boulder, CO and London, 1995.

Metcalf, Barbara, ed. *Moral Conduct and Authority: The Place of Adab in South Asian Islam*. Berkeley, CA, 1984.

Moosa, Ebrahim. 'Muslims ask: Does cloning distort Creation?', *Voices Across Boundaries* (Canada), vol.1:2 (2003–4), pp. 34–37.

Nafisi, Azar. *Reading Lolita in Tehran: A Memoir in Books*. New York, 2003.

Nanji, Azim. 'The Ethical Tradition in Islam,' in A. Nanji, ed., *The Muslim Almanac*. New York, 1996, pp. 205–11.

Nasr, Seyyed Hossein. 'Islam and the Environmental Crisis,' in S. Rockefeller and J. Elder, ed., *Spirit and Nature: Why the Environment is a Religious Issue*. Boston, MA, 1992, pp. 83–108.

Ozdalga, Elisabeth and S. Persson, ed. *Civil Society, Democracy and the Muslim World*. Istanbul, 1997.

Peterson, Anna L. *Being Human: Ethics, Environment, and Our Place in the World*. Berkeley, CA, 2001.

Rachels, James. 'The Ethics of Virtue and the Ethics of Right Action,' in *Elements of Moral Philosophy*. New York, 1978, pp. 157–79.

Rahman, Fazlur. *Islam and Modernity: Transformation of an Intellectual Tradition*. Chicago, IL, 1982.

Rawls, John. *Lectures on the History of Moral Philosophy*, ed. Barbara Herman. Cambridge, MA, 2000.

Rispler-Chaim, Vardit. *Islamic Medical Ethics in the Twentieth Century*. Leiden, 1993.

Runzo, J. and N. Martin, ed. *Ethics in the World Religions*. New York and Oxford, 2001.

Sachedina, A. 'Islamic perspectives on research with human embryonic stem cells,' in National Bioethics Advisory Commission, *Ethical Issues in Human Stem Cell Research, Religious Perspectives*. Rockville, MD, 2000, vol. 3, pp. G1–G6.

—— *The Islamic Roots of Democratic Pluralism*. New York, 2001.

Sadri, M. and A. Sadri, ed. *Reason, Freedom and Democracy in Islam: Essential Writings of Abdolkarim Soroush*. Oxford, 2000.

Sajoo, Amyn B. *Pluralism in Old Societies and New States*. Singapore, 1994.

—— 'The Islamic Ethos and the Spirit of Humanism,' *International Journal of Politics, Culture and Society*, 8 (1995), pp. 579–96.

—— 'Ethics in the Civitas,' in A.B. Sajoo, ed., *Civil Society in the Muslim World*. London, 2002, pp. 214–46.

Salvatore, Armando and D.F. Eickelman, ed. *Public Islam and the Common*

Good. Leiden, 2004.

Sandel, Michael J. 'The Case Against Perfection,' *The Atlantic Monthly*, vol. 293:3 (2004), pp. 50-62.

Sen, Amartya K. *Development as Freedom*. New York, 1999.

Shanner, Laura. 'Stem Cell Terminology: Practical, Theological and Ethical Implications,' *Health Law Review Papers – Symposium of September 21, 2002* (University of Alberta Stem Cell Task Force), pp. 62–66; *http://www.stemcellnetwork.ca/news/features/billc13/hlr.php*

Somerville, Margaret. *The Ethical Canary: Science, Society and the Human Spirit*. London and Toronto, 2000.

Sumner, L.W. and J. Boyle. *Philosophical Perspectives on Bioethics*. Toronto, 1996.

Tamimi, Azzam and J.L. Esposito, ed. *Islam and Secularism in the Middle East*. London, 2000.

Tapper, Richard. *The New Iranian Cinema: Politics, Representation and Identity*. London, 2002.

Taylor, Charles. *The Ethics of Authenticity*. Cambridge, MA, 1991.

——'Sacred Killing,' *Voices Across Boundaries*, 1:1 (2003), pp. 11–16.

Tibi, Bassam. *Islam between Culture and Politics*. New York, 2001.

al-Tusi, Nasir al-Din. *The Nasirean Ethics*, trans. G.M. Wickens. London, 1964.

United Nations Development Program (UNDP), 'Liberating human capabilities: governance, human development and the Arab world,' *Arab Human Development Report 2002*. New York, 2002, pp. 105–120.

Vahdat, Farzin. 'Post-Revolutionary Islamic Discourses on Modernity in Iran: Expansion and Contraction of Human Subjectivity,' *International Journal of Middle East Studies* (November, 2003), pp. 599–631.

Visser, Margaret. *Beyond Fate: The 2002 Massey Lectures*. Toronto, 2002.

Walzer, R. *Al-Farabi on the Perfect State*. Oxford, 1985.

Watt, W. Montgomery. *Muhammad at Medina*. Oxford, 1956; repr., 1977.

Williams, Bernard. *Ethics and the Limits of Philosophy*. Cambridge, MA, 1985.

Zubaida, Sami. *Law and Power in the Islamic World*. London, 2003.

Index

'Abd al-Raziq, 'Ali 37
Abel 63
abortion 13–16, 113
Abou El Fadl, Khaled 4, 89
adab 1, 2, 3, 35, 85, 88, 91
adl 42
Afghanistan 39, 41, 45, 67, 74, 78, 83, 86, 87, 88, 93
Aga Khan 23, 87, 99, 107
Aga Khan Development Network (AKDN) 23, 99–107
Aghajari, Hashem 65, 80, 81
ahl al-kitab 91
akhlaq 10, 11, 35, 85, 88, 91
Akiner, Shirin 67
Algeria 37, 39, 41
'Ali ibn Abi Talib 73, 102, 103, 104
Alzheimer's disease 12, 20
Andalusia 57, 61, 62
Anderson, Jon 68
Ankara 39
An-Na'im, Abdullahi 34, 88
apartheid 81
Aquinas, St Thomas 21
Aristotle, Aristotelian 2, 5, 6, 21, 27, 35, 60, 61
Arkoun, Mohammed 4, 34, 88

Armenia 38
Armstrong, Karen 56
Asad, Talal xii
Ash'aris 61
Avignon 61
Azerbaijan, Azerbaijanis 37, 38, 39
al-Azm, Sadeq Jalal 34, 87

Badakhshan 67
Badawi, Sheikh Zaki 52
Baghdad 10, 61, 102
al-Baghdadi, 'Abd al-Latif 10
al-Battani, Abu 'Abd Allah Muhammad 61
Berlin 28
Bhagavad Gita 3
bioethics 13, 17, 19
bin Laden, Osama 53
al-Biruni, Abu al-Rayhan 103
Bobbio, Norberto 61
Bosnia 37, 82, 86, 93
Bowling Alone (Putnam) 28
Le Bouc emissaire (Girard) 55–56
Britain *see* Great Britain
Brussels 74
Bukhara 102
Bunt, Gary 68

Bush, George 50

Cain 63
Cairo 10, 61, 62, 102, 106
Canada 48, 69, 78, 79, 81, 82, 84, 89
Canadian Broadcasting Corporation (CBC) 52
Carothers, Thomas 32
Carter, Stephen 70, 88
Casanova, Jose 69, 89
Catholics, Catholic church 13, 47, 48, 65, 82
Central Asia 38, 39, 62, 65, 71, 82, 105
Chadwick, Owen x
Charter of Medina 73, 94
China 102
Christians, Christianity 3, 10, 21, 23, 29, 30, 51, 53, 55, 56, 57, 62, 63, 69, 76, 83, 84, 85, 90, 110
Church and State 74, 79
citizenship 26, 29, 30, 31, 32, 38, 40, 49, 66, 69, 71, 75, 80, 81, 84, 89, 91, 92
civic culture 24, 25, 28–34 *passim*, 38, 41, 43, 44, 45, 49, 69, 74, 75, 76, 78, 85, 88
civic ethics 65, 66, 85, 89
civility 18, 25–46 *passim*, 50, 57, 63, 75, 76, 77, 81, 83, 85, 86, 92
civil society 6, 23, 25–45 passim, 62, 67, 68, 70, 71, 73, 74, 76, 78, 81, 82, 83, 85, 86, 88, 90
civitas 26, 44, 45, 46, 47, 93
'clash of civilizations' 30, 44, 49, 53, 74, 83, 90
The Clash of Civilizations (Huntington) 51, 83
Cluny 61
cloning 15–16, 20

Cold War 32, 43, 67, 74, 86
communitarianism 29–30, 101
Cordoba 61, 62, 9z, 102
Crick, Bernard 12
Croatia 82
Crusades, Crusaders 56, 57

'discourse ethics' 31, 45
al-Dakhwar 10
Dallal, Ahmad 10
Damascus 10, 145
Dar al-'Ilm 102
dar al-harb 52
dar al-Islam 10, 52
Davari, Reza 63
dawla 25, 34, 45
Defoe, Daniel 60
Delhi 62
democracy 34, 41, 73, 74, 82
Deuteronomy 56
Development and Justice Party (AKP) 66
devlet baba 39
dhimmi 91
din and *duniya* 13, 34, 45, 77, 99, 100
see also sacred and secular
Durkheim, Emile, Durkheimian 45, 47, 49, 58
Dworkin, Ronald 70

Eastern Europe 52, 82
Ecole de Technologie Superieure 79
Egypt 36, 65, 87, 90
Eickelman, Dale 31, 68
Enishte 90
Esposito, John 31
Ethics and the Limits of Philosophy (Williams) 6
ethnicity 33, 75, 89
Etzioni, Amitai 29, 30, 89

Euclid 103
euthanasia 13, 16–17, 20

Falk, Richard 43, 89
al-Farabi, Abu al-Nasr 2, 26, 35, 60, 62
Faradov, Tair 38
Farmanara, Bahman 66
Fatimid dynasty 61, 62, 90, 102
fatwas 15, 125
Ferguson, Adam 74
fiqh 2, 10, 14, 23, 64, 65, 68
Formations of the Secular (Asad) xii
France 61, 68, 69, 89, 93
Fraser, Nancy 91–92
The Future of Freedom (Zakaria) 82
The Future of Human Nature (Habermas) 7

Galen, Galenic 10, 103
Gandhi, Mahatma 21
Gellner, Ernest 28, 30–31, 88
Germany 68, 89, 93
al-Ghannouchi, Rachid 34
al-Ghazali, Abu Hamid 2, 10, 14, 35, 60, 61, 62, 103, 109
Giddens, Anthony 29
Gilgamesh, Epic of 3
Girard, René 55–56, 90
globalization 23, 27, 33, 49, 67, 68, 70, 84, 89
Goodman, Lenn 54
governance 23, 28, 72–93, 101, 106
Gray, John 29, 70
Great Britain 68, 82, 89, 143
Gross, Nasrine 67
Grotius 85
Gulf War 86
Güllen, Fethullah 66
Gutenberg, Johann 61

Habermas, Jürgen 7, 8, 31, 45
Hadith 3, 10, 22, 35, 42, 55, 91
Hafiz 53
al-Hakam II 61
Halevi, Judah 57
Haq, Nomanul 2
Harvard University 80
Haseltine, William 12
Hashmi, Sohail 4, 55
What Went Wrong? (Lewis) 51
Havel, Vaclav 28, 86, 88
Hayy Ibn Yaqzan 3, 60, 62
Hebrew 3
Heclo, Hugh 88
Hegel, Georg 74
Hellenistic 10
Heraklius 56
hilm 42, 61
hima 22, 130
Himmelfarb, Gertrude 29, 44, 70
Hindus, Hinduism 90
Hiroshima 51
History of Science (Sarton) 103
Homer 3
honour killing 66
Hourani, George 58
Hroswitha of Gandersheim 62
hukm 73, 91, 138
humanism 5, 47, 73
Human Genome Project 12
human rights 8, 12, 13, 26, 28, 29, 32, 40, 41, 44, 45, 49, 64, 65, 66, 69, 70, 74, 79, 84, 85, 87, 88, 92, 93
Huntington, Samuel P. 30, 49, 50–51, 53, 56, 83, 84

Ibn Abi Usaybia 10
Ibn al-Baytar, Diya' al-Din 10
Ibn 'Arabi, Muhyi al-Din 21
Ibn al-Haytham, Abu 'Abd Allah

61, 103
Ibn Hunanyn 35
Ibn al-Jawzi, Abu'l Faraj 37
Ibn Khaldun, 'Abd al-Rahman 62
Ibn Khallikan, Ahmad b.
  Muhammad 103
Ibn al-Nafis, 'Ala al-Din 10, 11, 61
Ibn Rushd (Averroes) Abu al-Walid
  Muhammad 2, 5, 26, 60, 62
Ibn Sina (Avicenna) Abu 'Ali al-
  Husayn 60, 61, 103, 105
Ibn Taymiyya, Taqi al-Din 22, 62
Ibn Tufayl, Abu Bakr Muhammad
  60
Ibrahim, Saad Eddin 87
Ignatieff, Michael 85
ihsan 42
ijtihad 36, 62
Ikhwan al-Safa 59
Imam, Ayesha 87
individualism 17, 29, 33, 70, 83, 93
Indonesia 37, 84, 87, 93
Iqbal, Mohammad 103
Iran 31, 36, 39, 40, 43, 65, 66, 69, 83,
  87–88
Iraq 37, 45, 51, 72, 73, 78, 83, 84, 86,
  88
Islamic Code of Medical Ethics 16–17,
  108–116
Islam and Human Rights (Mayer) 64
Israel 56, 57, 112
Istanbul 62
istihsan 12

al-Jabri, Mohamed Abdel 34
Jerusalem 56, 57, 143
Jews, Jewish 51, 53, 56, 57, 62, 63, 76,
  81, 84, 90, 91, 93, 95, 96, 97
jihad 42, 52, 53, 54, 56, 80, 90
Johnson, James Turner 55

Jordan 65, 66, 69
Judaeo-Christian 10, 89
Judaism 57, 69, 91

Kadivar, Mohsen 87
kalam 5
Kalila wa Dimna 3
Kant, Immanuel 1, 8–9
Keane, John 28, 33, 34
Kelsay, John 55
Khatami, Muhammad 80
Khudanazarov, Daulat 66, 67, 87
al-Khwarizmi, Muhammad b. Musa
  61
Kiarostami, Abbas 65
Kierkegaard, Søren 1, 24
al-Kindi, Abu Yusuf Ya'qub 60, 102
al-Kirmani, Hamid al-Din 60, 62
Kosovo 78, 82, 86, 93
Kramer, Martin 51
Kung, Hans 89
Kurds 39
Kuttner, Robert 29

laicité see secularism
Lebanon 37
Lefebure, Leo 56, 143
Lewis, Bernard 34, 51–53, 54, 56, 62
liberalism 6, 8, 27, 29, 47, 49, 88, 89
Locke, John 74

MacIntosh, Douglas 47–48
MacIntyre, Alasdair 4, 5
al-Madina al-fadila (al-Farabi) 62
Madjid, Nurcolish 34
madrassas 39
Mahfouz, Naguib 3
Maimonides 57
Majidi, Majid 65
Majlis al-Hukm (Council of

Governance) 73
al-Majusi, 'Abbas 10
Makhmalbaf, Mohsen 65
Makhmalbaf, Samira 66
Manas, Epic of 3
Maqamat (al-Hariri) 3
maslaha 11, 12, 15, 16
al-Mawardi, Abu al-Hasan 60
Mayer, Ann Elizabeth 64
Mazrui, Ali 89
McClay, Wilfred 53, 69, 88
McLachlin, Beverley 70–71, 84–85, 88
Medina 26, 58, 63, 73, 75, 94, 98, 104
Mediterranean 35, 61
Menocal, Maria Rosa 62
Mernissi, Fatima 88
Mill, John Stuart 85
Miskawayh, Ahmad ibn Muhammad 2, 10, 35, 60
Mizan al-'amal (al-Ghazali) 35, 61
modernity 17, 30, 31, 37, 45, 47, 50, 51, 53, 54, 57, 63, 68, 73, 74, 85, 88, 89
Moosa, Ebrahim 4
Moralities (Smith) 29
Mowatt, Don 52
Mu'tazilis 60, 61
Mughal India 22, 90
Muhammad, the Prophet 2, 19, 22–23, 26, 52, 55, 58, 63, 73, 75, 76, 81, 91, 100, 101, 102, 104, 105, 110, 112
Muhammad Ali 48
Muqaddima (Ibn Khaldun) 62
Muzaffar, Chandra 34, 87
My Name is Red (Pamuk) 90

nafs 24, 42, 52, 76
Nagasaki 51

Nasir-i Khusraw 102
The Nasirean Ethics (Akhlaq-i Nasiri of al-Tusi) 35, 61
neo-Platonism 35, 60
Netherlands 68, 69, 89
Neuhaus, Richard 88
New York 52, 74, 79
Nicomachean Ethics (Aristotle) 35
Nigeria 39, 65, 69, 87
Niyazi, Aziz 66
Noah's ark ix–x, xi
Noor, Farish 87
Northern Ireland 82, 83
North Africa 57
North America 17, 47, 48, 49, 68, 79, 83, 93
Nuh ix–x *see also* Noah's ark
Nurcu movement 66
Nursi, Bediüzzaman Said 66

Ontario 48, 80
Ottoman Empire 90

Pakistan 36, 65, 69
Palestine 41
Pamuk, Orhan 3, 90
Panahi, Jafar 66
Philippines 43
Pipes, Daniel 51
Plato 62
pluralism 24, 26, 29, 33, 40, 44, 45, 48, 51, 54, 57, 62, 63, 73–93 *passim*
Popper, Karl 28
Protestantism 69
Ptolemy 103
public ethics 29, 67, 81
Pufendorf, Samuel von 85
Putnam, Robert 28, 29, 70

al-Qaeda 142

Quebec 48, 79, 80, 81, 82, 83, 149
Qanun fi'l-tibb (Ibn Sina) 61
Qur'an 2, 3, 4, 22, 35, 42, 54, 55,
    58–59, 60, 63, 64, 65, 72, 76, 77,
    80, 81, 88, 90, 91, 101, 102, 103,
    104, 105, 110, 112

Rahman, Fazlur 4, 10, 34, 63, 91
Ramadan, Tariq 88
Rasa'il of the Ikhwan al-Safa' 59
rationes legis 36
Rawls, John 47
Raymund of Aguiles 56
al-Razi (Rhazes), Abu Bakr
    Muhammad 2, 103, 105
religion and state 74, 77, 80, 81, 87,
    88, 89
Religion Returns to the Public Square
    (Heclo and McClay) 53, 88
Republic (Plato) 62
Ricoeur, Paul 40
Robinson Crusoe (Defoe) 60
Rorty, Richard 27, 33
rule of law 10, 24, 25, 29, 30, 31, 32,
    37, 38, 40, 41, 44, 45, 49, 64, 67,
    70, 71, 72–88 *passim*, 92
Rumi 53
Rumsfeld, Donald 55

Sachedina, Abdulaziz 89
sacred and secular 2, 3 42–43, 45,
    47, 77, 88, 89–90 *see also din* and
    duniya
Sadawi, Nawal 87
Saddam Hussein 45
Saladin 56, 61
Salih, Tayib 3
Salut, Shaykh
Samar, Sima 67, 87
Samarqand 102

Sana'i 103
Sandel, Michael 29, 70, 89
SARS 79, 149
Sarton, George 103
satyagraha 21
Saudi Arabia 15, 36, 65, 83
Saul, John Ralston 28, 29
Scandinavia 68
Scottish Enlightenment 27
secularism, secularization 32, 34, 37,
    43, 47, 48, 49, 63, 66, 69, 88, 89
Seligman, Adam 44
Sen, Amartya 89
Shahrur, Muhammad 65, 87
Shamir, Itzhak 57
Shari'a 10, 35, 36, 38, 39, 40, 53, 54,
    64, 65, 72, 73, 77
Shi'ism, Shi'is 14, 60, 65, 80, 86
Shils, Edward 75
Sikhs 79
Singh, Gurbaj 78
siyasa 36
Smith, Joan 29
social capital 38, 81
social equity 40, 82
social ethics 27–31 *passim*, 35, 37, 38,
    40, 44, 45, 74, 85
Socrates 5
Somalia 37
Somerville, Margaret 15
Soros, George 28
Soroush, Abdolkarim 1, 4, 24, 34,
    37, 65, 87
Soueif, Ahdaf 3
South Africa 71, 81
South America 48, 51, 52
Soviet Union 82
Spain 22, 60, 62, 82, 83
Sudan 37, 39
Sufism, Sufis 53, 60, 61, 62

Summers. Larry 80
Sunni Islam, Sunnis 61, 84, 86
Supreme Court (Canada) 79;
    (United States) 48, 76
Syria 65, 87

Tahafut al-falasifa (al-Ghazali) 61
Tahdhib al-Akhlaq (Miskawayh) 35
Tajikistan 23, 37, 66, 67, 78, 82, 86,
    87
Taliban 45, 78, 147
taqlid 4, 36
taqwa 60, 63, 81, 88
*tariqa*s 21
Taylor, Charles 27, 30, 49, 56, 70, 89
The Right and the Good (Ross) 85
Thompson, E.P. 32
Tibi, Bassam 34, 45
Tito, Josip Broz 82
Tocqueville, Alexis de 49, 76
Torah 57
Toronto 79
totalitarianism 33, 82
Turkey 31, 38, 39, 65, 66, 69, 84, 90,
    93
al-Tusi, Nasir al-Din 2, 8–9, 10, 35,
    60

ulama 36, 64
ulm al-nafs 24, 42
'Umar, caliph 18, 21, 72, 115
umma 2, 4, 5, 18, 21, 24, 25, 30, 31,
    35, 42, 45, 46, 58, 61, 63, 68, 73, 75,
    76, 77, 89

United Nations 40, 86
United States 47, 48, 53, 69, 78, 81,
    82, 83, 86
University of Chicago 47
Upanishads 3
Uzbekistan 82

Vassanji, M.G. 3
velayat-e faqih 36, 81
Vietnam War 48
Visser, Margaret 44, 70

Wadud, Amina 89
wahdat al-wujud 21
Wahid, Abdulrahman 87
Walzer, Michael 70
*waqf*s 39
Washington 48, 74
Watson, James 12
weltanschauung 34, 37, 44
Western Europe 17, 69
Williams, Bernard xii, xiii, 6, 7
Wilmut, Ian 15, 126
Wolff, Christian 85
World Health Organization 79

Yale University 47
Yasin, Ziyad 80, 81
Yusuf, Hamza 88

Zakaria, Fareed 82
zakat 39
Zen Buddhism 21
zulm 42